COMPLETING YOUR
DOCTORAL DISSERTATION
OR MASTER'S THESIS

SECOND EDITION

Completing Your Doctoral Dissertation or Master's Thesis

in two semesters or less

DR. EVELYN HUNT OGDEN

TECHNOMIC PUBLISHING CO., INC.

LANCASTER • BASEL

Completing Your Doctoral Dissertation or Master's Thesis
a TECHNOMIC publication

Published in the Western Hemisphere by
Technomic Publishing Company, Inc.
851 New Holland Avenue, Box 3535
Lancaster, Pennsylvania 17604 U.S.A.

Distributed in the Rest of the World by
Technomic Publishing AG
Missionsstrasse 44
CH-4055 Basel, Switzerland

Main entry under title:
  Completing Your Doctoral Dissertation or Master's Thesis:
    In Two Semesters or Less—*Second Edition*

A Technomic Publishing Company book
Bibliography: p.

Library of Congress Card No. 93-60088
ISBN No. 1-56676-035-6

In memory of my advisor Peter A. Taylor, Ph.D.
who was both Professor T and Professor D

and

To future and current graduate students
and to those who have dropped out
but are willing to give it one more try,
this book is dedicated to evening the odds
between the student and university.

CONTENTS

LISTS, TESTS, FORMS, AND CHARTS

ACKNOWLEDGEMENTS

I wish to thank Elizabeth Casey and Diana Robinson, who spent many hours reading and editing drafts and making recommendations.

I also wish to thank the doctors, Ph.D.W.D.'s, and Ed.D.A.B.D.'s who shared with me profiles of their advisors and committee members and some of the "horror" stories of their dissertation experiences. For obvious reasons their contributions must remain anonymous.

I also wish to thank the doctors of philosophy and education who encouraged me to write this book. It was a privilege to work with them on their dissertations. Each project was a learning experience for me and I thoroughly enjoyed being involved.

INTRODUCTION

Dr. _____ (insert your name) or Mr., Miss, Mrs., Ms. _____ (insert your name), what will be your title? Every year thousands of the more than one million graduate students in the U.S. complete course work, qualifying exams, and dissertations and are awarded doctorates. Many of the completers complain bitterly of the months and years spent laboring over their dissertations. However, it is estimated that as many as 50% of doctoral-level students complete their course work but never complete the "write of passage." They become the Ph.D.W.D's (Doctor of Philosophy Without Dissertation) or Ed.D.A.B.D's (Doctor of Education All But Dissertation), a state in life as useful as almost surviving an operation. Anyone who is admitted to graduate school, completes the course work and passes the qualifying exam can write a successful dissertation; moreover, the experience need not be painful nor the operation long. You can do the actual writing in twenty days, and the planning, proposal development, data collection, data analysis, and defense in another thirty days. You can complete the process in fifty workdays (twenty-five weekends) over two semesters (see proposed time line on page xviii), you can work for a living, and you can continue your social life. You can produce a quality dissertation or thesis.

Skeptical? Try one of these exercises. If you are an employed graduate student, pull out all the memos, letters, and reports you have done in conjunction with your job in the past month. Next, add the last two or three course papers you have written. Put them in a pile. Pretty thick, isn't it? About the length of a decent dissertation: 100 pages (appendices not included). If you are a full-time graduate student, collect the last five or six papers you have written. On the back, in pencil (you may want to erase the evidence), write the number of hours you *really* spent writing the paper. Exclude time for coffee breaks, time complaining about writing the paper, and time daydreaming. Are the papers taken together 100 pages? Did the total writing time exceed 140 hours, or twenty seven-hour workdays?

Hopefully, you now agree that you can write 100 pages in twenty days. A dissertation is certainly more than a pile of memos and end-of-course papers, but it doesn't need to take more "real work" time to write. A dissertation is the proof that you have made the "rite of passage" from student to scholar by the production of credible research in your field. The important word in this definition is "credible." A dissertation is not the great American novel. The plot is almost certainly dull. When was the last time you read a dissertation for pleasure? Have you ever read a dissertation? Even in your field of study, your dissertation will not add great new insights. It will add one very small credible piece to the incremental development of knowledge in your field. It should not be the last piece of research you contribute to your field, but the first in your new professional life.

If a dissertation is, in fact, just a straightforward example of very limited research written in a simple style, then why are there so many Ph.D.W.D.'s and Ed.D.A.B.D.'s? Why are there so many horror stories connected to writing dissertations? The reasons for prolonged pain and, in too many cases, failure include:

- failure to get your head on straight about what a dissertation is and is not
- panic and paralysis from listening to and believing the horror stories
- failure to recognize the dissertation as a "rite of passage," as well as a "write of passage"
- lack of guidance and training in how to design and plan a dissertation
- selection of the wrong advisor or committee
- selection of the wrong topic
- failure to get the right help
- failure to invest money to save money
- failure to take charge of the project

This book will guide you through advisor/committee and topic selection, proposal development, data collection, data analysis, writing, editing, and defense of your dissertation. It is equally useful to publish-or-perish professors or those working on master's theses. It will lead you around the pitfalls of "head games," topic selection, advisors, committees, and yourself. It will help you navigate both the "write" and "rite" of passage. You will find as you travel through the book that your dissertation need not be a long painful interruption in your life, but a relatively short, tolerable experience with many rewards and controlled costs. The sample time line on page xviii illustrates how major dissertation activities fit into a TWO-SEMESTER work plan (if you have the luxury of more time or there is a longer wait-time for experimental results, then you can spread the workdays over a longer time frame).

When Is the Best Time to Use This Book?

1. Before you apply to graduate school
2. During your early course work
3. At the time when you are ready to begin your dissertation or thesis
4. When you are already in the dissertation game
5. When you are ready to defend your dissertation or thesis
6. When you are about to give up
7. When you have given up
8. ALL OF THE ABOVE

How to Use This Book

The book is laid out in sequential chapters, starting with getting oriented to the dissertation process (the process also can be applied to writing a master's thesis) and ending with the psychological problems associated with actually graduating. However, in order to maximize the efficiency of your work, you should read through the entire book once before you start. This will give you a holistic view of the process. In addition, there are various steps in the process and forms designed to facilitate your progress,

The Two-Semester Time Line of Activities

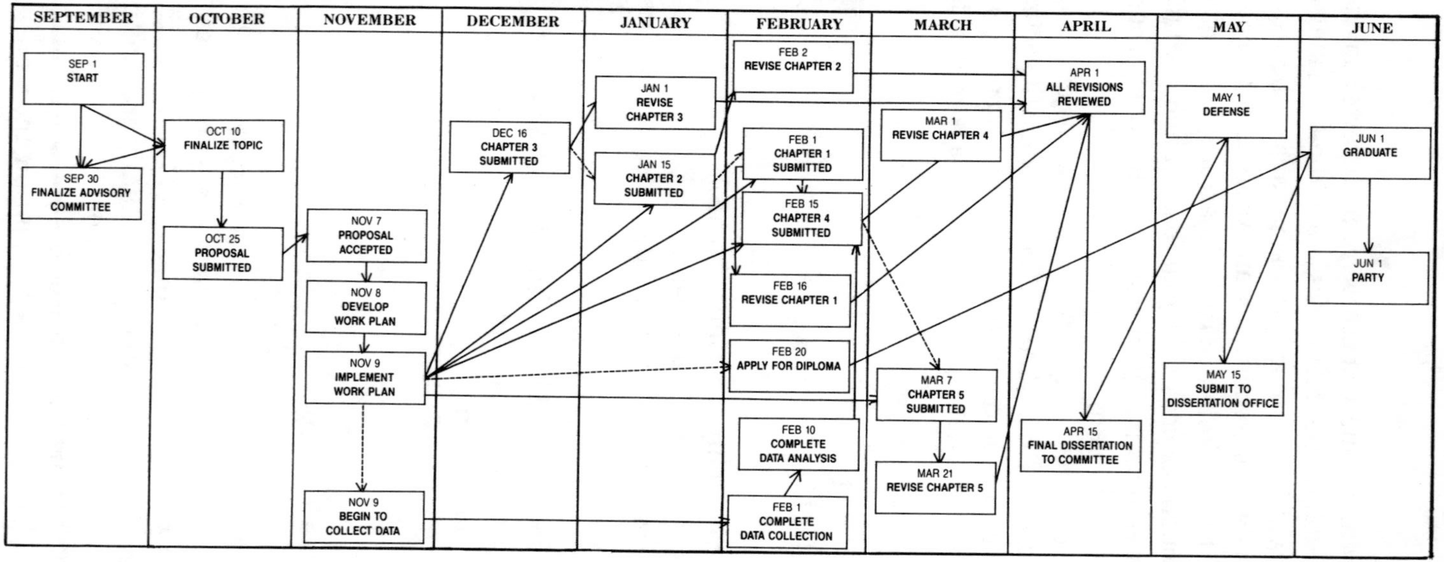

which appear in different chapters but which should be worked on at the same time. For example, while you are conducting research on advisors (Chapter 2) in the library, you can also be developing a list of acceptable dissertation topics (Chapter 3), beginning to develop the various sections of your dissertation proposal (Chapter 5), and analyzing the anatomies of dissertations (Chapter 6). The pragmatic idea is to work smart, not long.

CHAPTER 1

THE DOCTORAL DEGREE FACTS OF LIFE—THE BEGINNING

The Odds of Success!

In 1989 there were 194,137 academic doctoral students in the United States; of those, only 35,759 were awarded degrees. It took the median doctoral student 7.2 years of enrolled time to earn the degree. However, for 45% of those students it took from EIGHT to SIXTEEN years (National Center for Educational Statistics 1991). In addition, it is estimated that nearly 50% gave up and dropped out along the way. Usually the dropouts were those who completed the course work and exams BUT NOT THE DISSERTATION. Actually, the word *dropout* is probably a poor descriptor, for in most cases the graduate student just drifted away into the ranks of Ph.D.W.D. or Ed.D.A.B.D. After years of working and paying for registration and dissertation credits, the university imposed time limit, usually seven years, ran out, and even with extensions, the student eventually just gave up. Obviously, most students get at least one time line extension, since the median registered time exceeds that of the imposed limit. Many times the extension requires the student to take additional courses or even retake the examinations. Why should it take so long? What is even more frightening than the statistics is a growing acceptance on the part of graduate students that the degree process should take up a major portion of their lives!

It is not only the cost of graduate school that is increased by the extended dissertation time line. For the graduate student whose goal is to join the academic life as a professor, the extended time working as a research or as a teaching assistant may provide real on-the-job training, even if such training is at poverty-level wages. However, for the majority (66%) of the graduates who enter or continue in the world of work outside of the academic walls, the extended time line means not only lost income, but a lengthy delay in potential career advancement (National Center for Educational Statistics 1990). Actually, if your goal is a doctorate and you are not too choosey about the field, your best shot is in medicine or law, where the usual time to the degree is four years and the successful completion rate is much higher than for an academic doctorate. What is the difference between academic doctorates and medical and legal doctoral degrees, which accounts for the huge difference in time commitment? It's certainly not intelligence; studies show that the average IQ of those awarded Ph.D.'s actually exceeds those of medical students and lawyers (Cronbach 1949, Ruck 1959). The difference is that lawyers and medical doctors do not have to write DISSERTATIONS.

The first academic doctorate was awarded by Yale in 1861. The requirements were two years of course work, an examination, and a written dissertation. The Association of Graduate Schools and the Council of Graduate Schools, in a joint statement, have reaffirmed these requirements.

> Normally the course of study leading to the doctorate: a year or two of lectures and seminars, followed by a general examination and a dissertation. The entire course of study should involve NO MORE THAN THREE, at most four years beyond the BACCA-LAUREATE. (Anderson 1992)

However, the median time to earn the degree has actually risen from 5.6 years in 1971 to 7.2 years in 1989. In the humanities the median has risen to 8.4 years and in education to 8.3 years. What has gone wrong in the past 130 years? If the requirements have not changed, then why does it now take four to thirteen years longer to complete the doctorate than in 1861? The course time and examination have changed very little. The kicker comes at the DISSERTATION stage. It should not take four to twelve years to write a dissertation. Yale in 1861 and the Association of Graduate Schools and Council of Graduate Schools in 1964 had it right, the DISSERTATION SHOULD TAKE ONLY ONE YEAR. It is no wonder that the average doctoral student has come to view the dissertation as the academic Mt. Everest WALL.

2

Winning the Game—Beating the ODDS!

The premise of this book is that you can successfully scale the DISSERTATION WALL in TWO SEMESTERS or less. This is a very REASONABLE EXPECTATION. It should be noted that, while the majority of students took more than seven years, 22% took only five years or less (National Center for Educational Statistics 1990). The following chapters debunk the myths, provide a step-by-step concrete approach for working smart, lay out strategies for avoiding and overcoming obstacles, and provide needed insights into the rites and write of passage. Understanding the process and the politics of the dissertation is a critical first step for every doctoral student, whether you are

- just contemplating entry into a doctoral program
- taking courses
- ready to start the dissertation process
- in the dissertation process
- bogged down in the dissertation process
- pretending you are still part of the process
- have dropped out of the process but are tempted to give it one more try
- about to defend your dissertation

Each stage in the journey has its opportunities and pitfalls. The goal of this book is to even the odds between the bureaucracy and power structure of the university and the individual graduate student. In order to successfully navigate the course, it is essential to understand the politics and the rites of passage, explode the myths, and confront self-imposed constraints. In other words, step one for those entering the process is to GET YOUR HEAD ON STRAIGHT; for those in the process, step one is to make sure that YOUR HEAD IS ON STRAIGHT and, if it is not, to take remedial action.

What a Dissertation Is

Let's take a look at what the graduate schools say a dissertation is. Based on a review of a number of graduate school handbooks and catalogue statements concerning doctoral degree requirements, two types of statements typify the descriptions of the dissertation.

1. Type 1–The dissertation is a scholarly work that represents one or more of the following types of research:
   - historical and philosophical
   - experimental
   - exploratory and descriptive

   The subject chosen must be definite and of limited range, the method of investigation must be exactly formulated, the value of sources must be established and the conclusion systematically supported.

2. Type 2–The student is required to prepare a dissertation under the guidance of a thesis advisor. The dissertation must be of such a caliber as to be acceptable for publication in a standard journal when suitably condensed.

Note the use of the words "limited," "definite," and "scholarly." Is it the "scholarly" that conjures up visions of unclimbable mountains? *Webster's New World Dictionary* defines scholarly as "orderly and thorough in method of study." You can be that, and, therefore, you can do a scholarly paper.

Haven't you done umpteen college papers that were "limited" and "definite"? Excluding papers you did on Sunday night for class on Monday, you have probably done a number of papers that were "orderly and thorough." So what is the big deal?

It is not a big deal. A dissertation is no more than an orderly and thorough piece of work, done on a limited topic related to what you have been studying, that demonstrates to a group of professors that you know how to undertake and report research. It can be 200 pages long (if you are nuts) or, in the case of some of the sciences, twenty pages long. A good committee will read, not weigh, your dissertation.

You have, by this time, been attending to your formal education on a full- or part-time basis for eighteen to forty years. Make a list of the dissertations you have read in full; abstracts do not count. Think of the most impressive professors you have had for courses.

What were their dissertation topics? Have you read their dissertations? List all the dissertations you have used as textbooks in courses. Are your lists short? As a matter of fact, the odds are that the paper is blank. Why is it then that, if dissertations are such a big deal, even those of noted scholars have so little visibility? The answer lies in what a dissertation is and is not.

The Dissertation Myths—"Once Upon a Time . . ."

The above points may sound logical, but many degree candidates start down the road to destruction at a very early point. There are many myths and tales circulating on campuses. Let's look at a few. There is the one about the student who had just finished his dissertation and went out to celebrate, only to return home to find his house burned to the ground and all of the copies of his dissertation gone. Then there is the one about the graduate student who was three pages from the end of the last chapter at the end of his seven years and was not granted an extension. Then there was the advisor who was deported to Canada shortly before the oral defense.

It is easy to begin to think of the dissertation as some mystical monster with a life of its own, whose mission is to defeat you. People who haven't even selected a topic have been heard to make statements such as, "I better take a year off from my job" or to ask such a question as, "Will I have to abandon my child if I start the dissertation now?" Such thoughts are paralyzing, counterproductive, and completely unrealistic.

What a Dissertation Is Not

Remember, a dissertation is a demonstration of your ability to do a limited research study of the caliber that appears in journals in your field. You are not being asked to find the cure for cancer or to write the great American epic. Nor do any of the dissertation requirements say that you have to have a burning interest in your topic. Sure, it is easier to work on something you find interesting; however, remember that the goal is to do a dissertation and graduate. If you strive for adequately non-boring and forget burning interest, you will be more apt to make the finish line.

Another important point to keep in mind is that, if you produce a really distinguished dissertation, you may contribute only a very small piece of knowledge to the overall understanding of your particular field. Read through several of the journals in your field. Note the limited scope of the published studies. Recognize and accept the notion that you will only contribute, at best, a minimum of knowledge through this exercise. After you get your degree, if you desire, you can devote your professional life to seeking the ultimate answers to the problems of the world. Now, the objective is to complete the research task as professionally, quickly, and painlessly as possible. Failure to see the dissertation in the perspective of an "exercise," a "demonstration" of your ability to do a credible piece of research, is often the first trap encountered by the student—a trap that can lead to degree death.

Finally, a dissertation is not a course requirement. There is an important difference between a dissertation and the other major papers you have written for courses. Course papers had to be completed by the end of the course. A course ends on a given day at a given hour. Failure to turn in the paper results in a lower or failing grade. If you have gotten this far, you must have had at least an acceptable pattern of meeting the course requirements. With a dissertation there is NO IMPOSED TIME LINE, other than that which a school may set for the total work on the degree, such as seven years. In the case of the dissertation, you can drift right up to the final school limit in years and no one will bug you. You can even drift right out of the program with little notice. With a dissertation you must take personal charge. Failure to recognize that the game has changed is the second fatal trap for graduate students.

Determining Your Dissertation Personality Quotient

Now that you have given some thought to what a dissertation is and is not, you may need to take a closer look at yourself.

Some of your ideas and traits will assist in the rapid completion of your dissertation, some will impede progress, and some will require action on your part. The following questionnaire is designed to help you get the task in perspective (it meets none of the requirements for instrumentation required in a thorough piece of research).

DISSERTATION PERSONALITY QUIZ

	YES	NO
1. I turned my course papers in on time.	☐	☐
2. I did my course papers because they were required and I didn't want to fail.	☐	☐
3. I did no more or no less than I thought was needed for the course.	☐	☐
4. I take courses because they are required, not for the love of learning.	☐	☐
5. I really like being a student.	☐	☐
6. I don't think of myself as a scholar.	☐	☐
7. I think my professors are more scholarly than I am.	☐	☐
8. I wait till the last minute to do a paper.	☐	☐
9. I can't really imagine myself writing a book.	☐	☐
10. The thought of using statistics scares me.	☐	☐
11. I am self-motivated.	☐	☐
12. I can't possibly think of a topic.	☐	☐
13. I hope I can pick an easy committee.	☐	☐
14. I have set a date for completing my dissertation.	☐	☐
15. I think I am different from my professors.	☐	☐
16. When I think about the dissertation, I see it as an obstacle.	☐	☐
17. I am afraid that I will fail.	☐	☐

If you answered yes to questions 1, 2, 4, and 12, you are typical. You are taking courses in order to get a degree, which in turn you hope will help you achieve some career goal. You may really enjoy some professors and courses, but you are there because it is a requirement. The standards for passing the courses are very clear, and you are usually confident that you can meet them.

If you look back, starting in first grade (or even kindergarten), this has been what formal education has been about. In the early years the objectives were clear and very short-range— "Complete problems 1 to 5 and then the class will go out to recess." College probably represented your first experience with semester objectives. The professor at the beginning of the semester told you what the course requirements were, including the paper topic, paper length, and due dates, and dates for midterms and finals. In many cases the professor did not mention the requirements again until just before each scheduled date. Semester planning was required on your part. If you didn't plan well, then you ended up doing "all nighters" at the end of the semester. Those in your freshman class who could not either adjust to the longer range objectives or plan their time disappeared by the end of the year.

The dissertation step is as different from your college and graduate courses as they, in turn, were different from your first grade experience. The time line is long since it can stretch over the one to four years left in the total number of years your graduate school allows for completion of the doctoral degree. In addition, it is usually possible to obtain an extension of time. There is little or no course content. You sign up for dissertation courses or seminars and pay your tuition, but in most cases you are not expected to produce anything specific, such as Chapter 2, as was the case in regular courses. You are expected to be planning, researching, and writing and to be "working" with your advisor; however, these are overly general expectations. Semesters and even years can go by while you tell people you are "exploring topics." In order to succeed in the dissertation game, you must see the differences and be able to play by new rules.

You have to establish the game plan, provide the motivation, and set and meet the deadlines. You have to substitute a set of extrinsic goals and incentives with an intrinsic set of goals and incentives, which you develop and monitor. You have to take charge.

If you answered yes to questions 5, 6, 7, 9, 10, and 15, then your mind-set is still that of a student. A doctorate signifies that the person has arrived at a level where he/she can make contributions to the field through research and teaching. When you enter the dissertation stage, you must start to think of yourself as a researcher and professor. When you finish your dissertation, you will know more about at least some small aspect of your field than anyone else. Your professors will be your colleagues. In most cases your career goal is not to be a college professor; however, the game is played in the graduate school and the other players are professors. Therefore, the game is the university's game!

The answers to the other questions will become apparent as you proceed through this book.

You Can Do It

Another self-imposed, possibly unrecognized problem can be a belief that professors, advisors, and others who have successfully completed dissertations are more capable than you are. In reality, can the difference between the survivors and the fatalities be intelligence? In fact, studies do show that Ph.D. candidates are brighter than medical and law students. But are all successful candidates brighter than you are? Can you have confidence in your ability? Try this exercise. On a piece of paper list all the people you know who hold a doctorate degree. Draw a double line and list all those people you know who have completed their course work and have not completed their dissertations. If you have trouble with the second list, make some tactful inquiries at work. You may be surprised at whom and how many are on your second list.

- Place one star next to the names of the people on your lists whom you think are brighter than you are.
- Place two stars next to the names of people whom you think are your equals in intelligence.
- Place three stars next to those whom you privately assess as dumber than you are.
- Place a check next to those whom you think will succeed in their careers.

This exercise should confirm a few things in your mind. One, people equally or less bright than yourself have jumped the dissertation hurdle. Two, brighter and equally bright people have failed in their attempts. Within limits then, intelligence is not the discriminating factor between the "do's" and the "I would have ifs . . .".

Understanding the Rite of Passage

The dissertation stage of your education is more than a time when you write a long research paper. It is also a complex rite of passage. Graduate schools admit many more doctoral-level students than degrees they expect to confer. Does this mean that graduate schools are merely scam operations, enticing clients into programs in which most are not expected to succeed? Where is truth in advertising? Does your graduate school publicize the ratio of students admitted to their programs and those awarded degrees? The answers to each of these questions is a probable "no."

Experience has shown that there is a considerable discrepancy between the number of graduate students admitted to programs and those that complete them. A study conducted at the University of North Carolina at Chapel Hill (Naylor and Sanford 1982) found that, after four years of doctoral study, only slightly more than half of the students who had not graduated were still enrolled. Since there is no certain way to predict who will be the completers and who will be the dropouts, schools need to admit relatively large numbers of students in order to

ensure that some will graduate. However, there are also con-
scious or unconscious gates built into the system to ensure that
not too many degrees are conferred. No school wants to be
known as a diploma mill. There is also a very practical reason
why graduate schools admit large numbers of students and
graduate few: it is called tuition. While tuition does not pay the
entire cost of the program, of necessity, it pays a substantial
share.

In order to offer a wide range of advanced courses, a large
number of students are required. The tuition that the many pay
contributes to the school both in terms of staff-lines allotted to
departments and to the ability to offer advanced courses with
low enrollment. Is this ethical? Certainly, you could argue that,
at best, it is a questionable practice. However, it can also be
argued that the schools admit those who have the potential to
succeed although they can't accurately predict who will actually succeed. Therefore, they provide equal opportunity and
leave success or failure up to the student. On the other hand,
few studies have been done by university faculty concerning the
characteristics of graduate completers and non-completers with
implications for initial student admission.

Unlocking the Doctoral Gates

The entrance exam may be the first gate. Theoretically, if you
pass this gate, you should be able to complete the program.
However, some schools let you take a number of courses before
you take the exam. The exam then results in a smaller pool of
students. Certain courses may also become gates that eliminate students from the pool. The comprehensive exams, written and/or oral, at the end or near the end of the course work,
are major gates or hurdles. The pool shrinks again. Finally,
there is the BIG GATE, the dissertation. What are the hazards
that add to the difficulty rating of this hurdle?

1. The school may have concerns about awarding too many doctoral degrees.

11

2. Professors may be rewarded by having their work with their advisees counted toward their work load; therefore, there is little incentive to have students graduate and be dropped from the count.

3. Professors may not be rewarded by having their work with advisees counted toward their work load; therefore, advising is just extra work.

4. Professors are professionals in academia. Except for the time defined by course schedules, professors are much less likely to be bound by the kinds of deadlines found in the non-academic work environment. Research in an area can take years, or even a professional lifetime. In many cases, the research is considered by the professor to be more important than teaching (the institution may also consider research the priority). The idea of a student wanting to rush through a research project to complete a degree and get out of academia is not easily appreciated by most professors.

5. Professors have made a career choice. They have chosen the academic environment; many have never worked outside of the university. They see the doctoral degree as entry into the world of scholarship, continuing research, and teaching, rather than as a ticket to careers outside their chosen environment.

6. Most professors like to study and to do research. They most probably liked studying and doing research when they were students. In many cases, they were full-time graduate students and spent a long time completing their dissertations.

7. Facilitating the graduation of a good research or teaching assistant may not be in the best interest of the advisor in terms of accomplishing his own work.

You have to recognize that these facts represent hazards. You and your professors may be standing at different ends of the elephant and therefore may be seeing or feeling the dissertation gate differently. You need to reflect on your school, department, major advisor, and professors. What makes them tick? What are their goals and objectives? How do they describe the elephant?

You must consider yourself as a candidate for their club. In order for you to be admitted, they must consider you ready. What constitutes ready? This is the part that is not in the school handbook. You have to understand the club, pick the right selection committee, and play the game. These are the rites of passage. How well you play the game will determine how long you have to play and if, in the end, you will win. You don't have to become a cynical phoney with a prepared script for every occasion; however, you have to be able to convince your advisors that your goals, objectives, and abilities are congruent enough with theirs that they are willing to consider you a colleague. The "passage" is from "me student—you professors" to "us colleagues." The rites are all the things you do to signal the professors that you have entered upon the passage and finally, with a successful oral defense of your dissertation, completed the journey.

Setting the Date for Your Oral Defense and Graduation

Remember that doing a successful dissertation in two semesters or less is a reasonable expectation. The first step then in developing a dissertation plan is to set your graduation date. This accomplished, you then begin to back down the time line. The oral defense usually has to be a given number of weeks prior to graduation. Set the date for your oral defense; be sure you have not picked a date during spring break. Note the date that you must apply for your diploma and the date the check is due. Review your school's time lines for other steps, which must be completed by a given time or in a given order. Make a list of the dates and key activities.

The Fifty-Day or Twenty-five-Weekend, Two-Semester Dissertation Schedule

With your graduation date set, begin to work backwards to figure the total time line. Figure that your dissertation in final

13

form probably needs to be submitted to your committee at least two weeks before the oral defense (check your manual or catalogue for the exact date). Estimate that your dissertation will be 100 pages long (a more exact method for establishing length will be covered in a later chapter). Writing at a rate of only one double-spaced page an hour, you will take 14.29 seven-hour days (three work-weeks or seven weekends) to write the dissertation. Figure revisions on one page in four, so add four more days. List dissertation writing as twenty days.

In addition, for conducting, collecting, and analyzing the data, add ten workdays; literature search and organization, add eight workdays; for writing your proposal, plan four workdays; for researching your committee, add two workdays; for selecting a topic, set four workdays; finally, for researching dissertation formats, add two workdays. These estimates are based on the experience of successful graduate students working seven-hour days. All daydreaming and stress attacks are excluded from the time estimates.

Adding up all the time-related activities from beginning to choose your topic to the end of the oral defense equals fifty days, or twenty-five weekends, or ten work-weeks, or some other combination of time. If you think you can write more than one double-spaced page an hour (remember this is straight writing, not creative prose) or if you have to have a particular advisor, then reduce the time estimate. Remember that these are seven-hour workdays, 3½ hours A.M., 1 hour lunch, 3½ hours P.M. If you work on the dissertation during the day, plan on enjoying the evening. If you work on the dissertation during the week, enjoy the weekend. All work and no play can lead to writer's block, breakdowns, or divorce.

Now spread the fifty workdays over two semesters. Remember, there will be considerable downtime while you are waiting for appointments, your advisor's comments, typist typing, meetings, and unexpected cancellations of meetings due to other commitments made by your advisor. Following is a sample list of major activities and completion dates for someone who starts in September and graduates in June (see also the two-semester time line in the Introduction). SET YOUR GRADUATION DATE AND WRITE IT DOWN and then read all of the chapters in this book, including the one on celebrating your degree, before you develop your time line. It is important to see the process holistically before zeroing in on the individual steps.

SAMPLE TIME LINE

Sept. 7	Complete researching completed dissertations
Sept. 15	Complete researching committee
Sept. 25	Complete preliminary literature and topic search
Sept. 30	Finalize advisor/committee
Oct. 10	Finalize topic
Oct. 25	Complete dissertation prospectus
Nov. 7	Proposal accepted
Nov. 8	Develop detailed work plan
Nov. 9 to Apr. 15	Implement plan and write dissertation
Feb. 20	Apply for diploma dated June
Apr. 15	Deliver final dissertation to committee
May 1	Oral defense
May 5	Dr. _____'s PARTY
May 15	Deliver revised final dissertation and abstracts to the dissertation office
June 1	GRADUATION
June 1	GRADUATION PARTY

Summary

This chapter has clarified what a dissertation is and is not. Personality and graduate school environmental factors that can impede progress of the dissertation were identified. The dissertation as a "rite of passage" as well as a "write of passage" was explored. It was calculated that a 100-page dissertation can be written by you in 14.29 days. A reasonable nine-month, two-semester start to graduation time line was suggested. A date was set for your graduation.

CHAPTER 2

RESEARCHING YOUR COMMITTEE— THE REALLY CRITICAL RESEARCH PROJECT

Your Choice/Their Choice

Your advisor and your committee members are THE most important pieces on the dissertation game board. This is where you make it or break it. With the RIGHT advisor you advance steadily around the board to collect your degree on schedule, proud of the work you have produced. With the WRONG advisor you will take every wrong route around the board, hit every dead end, advance one step only to fall back two steps, and continually run the risk of falling off the board completely, a Ph.D.W.D or Ed.D.A.B.D.

Researching your advisor and committee, therefore, is the MOST important research you will do concerning your dissertation. You do not always have a choice concerning your advisor. Your specific program may be so small that there is only one dissertation advisor, or your graduate school may assign advisors; however, you still need to do research in this area. The information you compile can help you to develop a strategy for working with the given advisor, or if the prognosis of success is bad enough, it may actually be worth switching to another department, even if you have to take a few more courses. Usually you have at least some flexibility in your selection. Since your options for selection of an advisor will have direct bearing on your selection of a dissertation topic, the chapter on researching advisors precedes the chapter on selecting a dissertation topic. There are thousands of topics in any field; however, you have a limited pool of advisors!

Researching your potential committee members is also a critical task. Your advisor will usually have major input into the decisions concerning committee membership, but if you are pre-

17

pared, you can propose potential members and effectively block other potential members.

This chapter treats the selection of advisor and committee members as if you had total freedom of choice and an unlimited pool of candidates for advisor and for committee membership. In the real world this will not be the case; however, knowing what sort of people to seek and what sort to avoid will help you to select the lesser of the evils and to develop strategies for achieving your goal with your real-life committee.

The Role of the Dissertation Advisor

In general, the role of the advisor is twofold: (1) to guide the candidate through the dissertation process and (2) to insure on behalf of the university, school, and department that the candidate is worthy of being granted a degree. This is not unlike the role of the real estate salesperson, who represents both the buyer and the seller, but whose major commitment must be to the seller.

Professors do not take courses on how to be dissertation advisors. Nor are there books on the role. Most professors teach the way they were taught and most professors advise the way they were advised. The culture of the individual university, school, and department plays a part in how the individual professor interprets the advisor/advisee relationship. Also, an individual's personality, including any hang-ups, affects his/her approach to the role.

Your advisor will have wide control over the dissertation process as you will experience it. He/she will approve your topic; will approve, if not select, your committee members; will approve your proposal; will or will not pay attention to your time lines; will approve every chapter, line, and conclusion in the dissertation; will determine when and how members of the committee will be involved in the dissertation process; will decide WHEN and IF you are READY to defend your dissertation; and in the end will determine whether or not you are granted the degree. Selection of your advisor should be done

18

with more care and knowledge than selecting a marriage partner. Divorce in the case of a marriage mistake can be easy compared to correcting an advisor mistake.

The Role of Dissertation Committee Members

The role of dissertation committee members is somewhat harder to define than that of the dissertation advisor. In general, their task is to give broader perspective on the development of the dissertation and to offer additional assurances to the university, school, and department that the dissertation standards have been met. In the specific sense, however, the membership role can vary greatly. In some cases their only involvement will be the reading of the dissertation after the advisor has approved the document, offering suggestions and criticisms, and participating in the defense meeting. In other cases, each committee member will actively contribute expertise at each stage of the dissertation process.

There are pluses and minuses to the models at both ends of the committee member involvement continuum. Involvement of the committee only after the completion of the dissertation simplifies the process during the development phases. There is only one person, the advisor with whom you are working, whose approval is needed to move to the next step. If your advisor is a truly powerful and respected member of the department and has selected or enthusiastically approved the other members of the committee, it is unlikely once he/she approves the dissertation that other members of the committee will cause problems for you or your advisor at the end of the process. If, on the other hand, your advisor is not all-powerful, not a heavy-weight in the field, and not highly respected by colleagues, waiting till the end of the process when the dissertation is completed before involving other members of the committee can be very bad news. Committee members may feel no ownership in the dissertation. They may not hesitate to tear apart the conclusions chapter, attack the topic itself, declare the literature support inadequate, and/or question the methodology. At the very least,

19

the late involvement approach concentrates the greatest power in the advisor, leaving the advisee no alternative but to trust the statements of the advisor. One final negative to the reduced role of the committee approach is that, if your advisor changes universities, falls out of favor within the political structure of the school or department, or dies during the dissertation process, there may be no one else who knows or cares about what you are doing.

The total committee involvement approach is at the other end of the involvement continuum. Usually the candidate working under this model will have major input into the selection of committee members. The advisor and advisee select members who will make specific contributions to the development and review of the dissertation. For example, one member may be selected because of strength in statistics and research design, another because the proposed topic involves an area of the field in which the member has expertise; another may be selected because of access to subjects needed for the study (even someone outside of the university). In this model, each member of the committee is directly involved from the beginning. The proposed topic is discussed with each potential member by the advisor and the advisee; potential members may help clarify or even modify the topic and general approach to be taken. If they agree to serve on the committee, they will already have bought into the dissertation. Each committee member will have input into each chapter of the dissertation and will approve each draft. Individual members will provide direct assistance to the candidate based on their areas of expertise. The advisor plays the role of chairperson of the dissertation team. The final defense of the dissertation becomes virtually a *pro forma* discussion and presentation, since each committee member has already approved every aspect of the dissertation prior to the defense.

There is, however, a downside to the involved-team model. It takes time to involve two to four additional people in each decision and in review of each chapter. Their individual comments and suggestions must be seriously addressed and, if not included in revisions, they will need to be approached in person.

20

Committee members may not agree with each other concerning changes. If one member of the committee flies off to Europe to do research or deliver a paper, you may have to wait before officially moving on to the next step. Under this model it may be difficult to stick to your time line.

In conclusion, there are two important questions to consider concerning committee member selection. First, what is the model of the committee membership involvement? In real life the specific model will probably not fall at the extremes, but somewhere to the left or right of center; the choice of advisor or school will determine the model to be followed. Second, what characteristics of committee members will be most effective for the actual model you will be working under?

The Non-Roles of the Advisor and Committee— Adjusting the Fantasy to the Reality

For some, the dissertation fantasy involves the graduate student working in a mentor relationship with a favorite professor. The professor considers working with the student his/her most interesting and important work, knows all the pitfalls, and selects committee members who are helpful and committed to the student and the topic. In addition, the professor knows all the school time lines and procedures and will accurately guide the student through the process. In this scenario, life is fair and so is the dissertation process!

For others, the dissertation fantasy is a nightmare of disjointed visions of sitting at a keyboard with hundreds of blank pages. The dissertation clock is ticking and a voice keeps saying, "You can't write a book," "You will never finish the degree," "You will fail, fail, fail." Your advisor is laughing at your ineptness.

Both of these fantasies are naive. Your advisor, assuming you made at least a reasonable choice, will be interested in your dissertation and in your success in navigating the process. However, advisors also teach classes, do their own research, write papers, and consult with other graduate students. You are only

21

one small part of their professional life. The advisor's expectation is that if you have reached the dissertation stage, you are capable of independently pursuing a bit of research. He/she is not there to hold your hand or to prod you like your mother did about cleaning your room. The advisor is there to offer guidance, to point out errors, to ensure that what you are doing meets the standards of the department and the advisor's personal standards. Your advisor has a reputation to protect, and since your completed dissertation will be presented to his/her colleagues, its quality will either enhance the advisor's reputation or lower credibility with those colleagues.

You need to look at the dissertation process from the advisor's and committee member's points of view. How much time is reasonable to devote to one student? What are the natural university cycles that influence interaction with students, i.e., examination schedules, vacations, due dates for grants the professor is working on, and personal research (publish or perish)? The advisor's work with advisees may count toward his/her work load, although this usually is not the case for committee members. What then do the members of the committee get out of the process? Usually not much other than added work. They may agree to be on your committee because (1) they take some interest in what you are doing; (2) they liked you when you were in their class; or (3) they owe your advisor a favor. The favor may be that your advisor served on a committee for one of their advisees. In addition, both advisors and committee members have personal lives that support or distract from their professional lives.

You need to get your expectations concerning the advisor/advisee relationship into perspective. Do your homework. Build a plan that fits the reality. If you can look at the process from both sides and adjust, you will not end up feeling rejected, and you will not take criticism personally.

The Good Advisor/Committee Test and Scoring Key

Understanding the roles of advisors and committee members is only the starting place. Making the right selection from the available pool of potential advisors and committee members involves several steps. Let's check your survival instincts. What follows is a list of advisor/committee member profiles. Take a minute and decide the potential of each professor as a good or bad candidate for advisor or committee member.

THE GOOD ADVISOR/COMMITTEE TEST

DESCRIPTION	GOOD	BAD
Prof T—He is in his office by 7A.M.—He meets with students every day—He has at least ten studies published each year—His is the most demanding research-related class given in the school.	☐	☐
Prof K—His courses are a snap—He never mentions research in class—He accepts practically any kind of paper—He gives almost all A's with an occassional B.	☐	☐
Prof Y—She is young and just finished her dissertation three years ago—She is very friendly with students—Everyone says that she is a "good guy."	☐	☐
Prof J—He is an old timer—He is head of the department—He has done and published research in one focused area for twenty years.	☐	☐
Prof D—Everyone has to take his stat course—Students and, privately, other professors quake when his name is mentioned—He is the guru of research and design—you worked like hell for a B in his course.	☐	☐
Prof I—He is an absolute leader in the field—He teaches only two classes—He is in constant demand as a consultant across the country.	☐	☐

Every professor has several characteristics that will add or subtract from his/her role as advisor; however, certain patterns of behavior should be weighed heavily in making a selection or in planning strategies for working with advisors. Let's look at each of the professors from the above test in terms of pros and cons. In each case the profile was based on one or more real advisors; however, the composites also represent a type.

Professor T

This professor is an outstanding candidate to be your advisor. If he successfully writes and publishes a study every month or two, he knows meaningful research can be produced in a short period of time. In the publish or perish environment of the university, his success in publishing will give him power. He obviously knows how to organize research, focus the topic, analyze the results, and draw conclusions. In describing the dissertation many universities use as a standard the production of a paper that would be acceptable to a major journal in the field. What faculty member would question Professor T's judgment that your dissertation meets this criteria? The fact that Professor T is in his office early every day also gives him high grades for advisor potential. You will be able to get to him on a regular basis. Finally, there is more than a little truth in the old saying, "If you want a job done, ask the busiest person you know."

In real life this advisor worked directly with the student to establish a written time line, provided guidance on topic selection, research design, statistical analysis, conceptualization, and literature review (including facilitation of direct contact with other "experts" in the field). The time from acceptance of the proposal by the committee to the time of the student's defense of the dissertation was less than three months.

Can there be a down side to a Professor T? Certainly. This type of very productive person expects others to be highly productive too. If you procrastinate, don't do your homework, or fall off your time line, you run the risk of being written off by a Professor T.

Professor K

This is the professor that most doctoral students gravitate toward as their advisor. Selecting this guy for the role will at least double your time line and drive you nuts. He is a major cause of Ph.D.W.D.'s and Ed.D.A.B.D.'s. He is laissez-faire about his courses. He spends little time preparing for class. He may even have the students prepare and present topics. His standards are vague and everyone who shows up passes. He doesn't like to do research, he does only the minimum to survive, he may actually reject formal research as irrelevant to real-life decisions in the field. As an advisor, he will not really care about your topic or your time line. He doesn't have the knowledge to be helpful in the design. He procrastinates with his own research, so he will not see a problem in taking extra weeks to look over a chapter you submit. He is likely to select other committee members who are also weak. Don't assume that in the end they will accept just "anything." Professor K and his committee may not do their homework along the route, but they will not hesitate in the latter stages suddenly to send you off in another direction or suggest a total rewrite.

In truth, a Professor K suggested topics that were almost impossible for the student to research (there was no way she could gain access to the population), recommended case studies rather than hypothesis-testing studies, and then, when the case studies were done, wanted to know how the student was going to test for significance. When he reviewed a chapter, which always took weeks, he would suddenly suggest that additional data might be "fun" to collect, requiring the student to go back to subjects already interviewed. He thought it was good to have committee involvement, but never got around to involving the committee until the end of the process. The committee members had many new suggestions. He was unclear about university time lines and, as a result, the student's actual graduation came close to being delayed for six months.

In another case, a Professor K was transferred to a university field site during the dissertation process. He was clearly not a power in his department. He lost every chapter that the student sent to him. Subsequent copies were sent, which he sat on for weeks or months before returning them to the student. As the student's deadline for completing the degree approached, he assured her that an extension was automatic. She completed the last chapter before the deadline; however, again he lost it. When he was sent another copy of the last chapter, there was another delay, and then when he did return the chapter, he had suggested changes. With the final changes all but completed, she ran out of time. The guaranteed extension promised by Professor K was not granted by the department. In order to continue she would have had to take additional courses and retake the qualifying exam. The result was that five years of full-time study and two years of work on a dissertation ended with a Ph.D.W.D.

An equally bad case of a Professor K type involved a truly brilliant biology student. After working for two years on his dissertation, with virtually no help from Professor K and many aggravating delays caused by Professor K, the student picked up a prestigious journal in his field and discovered his research in print under the name of the professor. It seemed that Professor K was being pressured by the university to publish more research and so he just took the student's work. When confronted by the student, he explained that all student work is the property of the professor and the student would have to start over. The university agreed with the professor who claimed that he had actually done most of the work and that the student's contribution had only been to carry out experiments under the direct supervision of the professor. Result— another Ph.D.W.D. and serious consideration given to murder.

Professor Y

This professor may seem like a good candidate. After all, she should understand the stresses and strains of dissertation writing. However, a young professor will be anxious to be accepted by the department hierarchy, may take care to study the time lines and mechanics of the dissertation process, but is unlikely to break with the long time line dissertation tradition rampant in most departments. Also, if a committee member suggests unreasonable changes or makes unreasonable recommendations, the young professor is unlikely to buck the more senior staff member. Finally, and this happens all the time, the young professor is unlikely to gain tenure, and, in many schools with an up-or-out philosophy, Professor Y may well end up working for another university before you finish your degree.

In real life, a Professor Y moved to a university across the country. No one else at the student's school was really interested in the student's research. The department agreed to let Professor Y continue as the advisor, but not the official advisor. Professor Y was still interested in the student's research and tried to be helpful. However, the pressure of her new job and the distance from the student made the process very difficult. Meanwhile, back at the ranch, the student's committee and new advisor viewed the student as a marginally acceptable step-child for whom any assistance represented a "favor." Desperate for assistance, the student contacted a consulting firm that advertised assistance to students. For a fee they offered help. They reviewed the completed first three and a half chapters, declared them disasters and offered to help the student for the fee of $40 a page. Shocked, but convinced that her dissertation was a mess, she stopped all work for a year. In fact, of the scores of dissertations I have read, this student's research design, care in collecting data, and writing skill displayed in the chapters represented one of the best pieces of work I have seen. With renewed confidence she completed her work and was awarded her degree. However, the price in terms of time and stress that she paid for selecting Professor Y as an advisor was tremendous.

Professor J

If you are interested in the same research area as Professor J, he may well be the advisor for you. He will have specific suggestions for topics and access to study populations. His colleagues know this is "his field" and they are unlikely to challenge him concerning research in his area. In addition, he has probably

27

worked with a slew of other students and knows who to put on a committee. However, if you are not interested in doing your dissertation on a topic suggested by Professor J or a topic you suggest related to his area, then forget him as a candidate for advisor. Typically, Professor J will find fault with every research topic outside of his area of interest. Even if you convince him to serve as your advisor with a topic of interest to you, he will be indifferent to your study and to you. Another potential downside to a Professor J can be his extreme interest in a topic in his area of research. It is not unusual for the Professor J's to keep adding to the research design or to the data analysis, even after the proposal has been accepted and the data collected. Professor J's continually think of questions they would like you to answer. They are more interested in the topic than in your desire to finish your dissertation. They obviously think research can and should go on forever; they have spent twenty years on their topics and are still able to come up with questions.

In real life, a Professor J was a particularly good choice for one student. The student had the greatest difficulty thinking of potential topics for his dissertation; he had no special area of interest. Professor J had several topic and research designs to suggest. The student picked one of the topics and received a great deal of assistance from Professor J throughout the process. Following his defense, which he described as a breeze thanks to Professor J's reputation with committee members, he and Professor J co-authored a journal article.

Another student who selected a Professor J made the wrong choice. She had aced Professor J's course and he had been very impressed with her research papers. He had predicted that she had a bright future as a professor and researcher if that was what she wanted to pursue as a career. Professor J was pleased to be her advisor. However, she had her own interests in research that were different from Professor J's. The student proposed several topics for study; however, Professor J found each unworthy of the student's efforts. Finally, after almost a year they agreed on a topic. But it was never an easy relationship. At each bend in the road Professor J tried to get the student to link her research to his interest; he found flaws in work already approved. He guided her to committee members whom he thought might be interested in "her topic" but for whom he had little respect. As a result, it was difficult to resolve differences among committee members concerning direction for the study or recommendations on drafts. Finally the student did complete the degree, but she did it the hard way.

Professor D

This type of professor should be given top consideration for committee membership. They can be a real help in formulating the hypotheses, designing, and analyzing your methods. Usually Professor D's do not have pet topics, so they are open to studies in any field. In terms of grades, a "B" from Professor D is like an "A" from other members of the department; therefore, Professor D will probably consider you at least an acceptable student. Finally, if Professor D accepts the design and approves the statistical applications, it is unlikely that anyone else on the committee will even mention these areas. In some departments, even if Professor D is not on a committee, he will be asked to review the design and analysis. It is better to get such input at the outset rather than at the end of the process.

In real life, a Professor D was a terrific committee member on many dissertation committees. In an hour he could help students formulate the correct wording for hypotheses, determine the sample size, guide them concerning procedures for collecting data, and select the appropriate statistics for analysis. He was tough but fair in class and he didn't waste time. He had the same approach to working with students on dissertations. When a student had a workable topic he was ready to help; however, he had no patience with students who had not done their homework and were groping for an idea. He was not a "hand-holder." He gave advice and he expected the student to follow that advice. The smart student did! He was so respected in the department that when one student turned in his dissertation with a typo, which showed several correlations greater than one, no one on the committee picked it up, meaning they hadn't even read the statistical analysis because Professor D had already approved the methodology. The student quietly changed the figures after the defense.

Professor I

This professor may be great for your career but bad as an advisor. However, based on your career goals, Professor I may or may not be worth the effort. In some fields the name of your advisor can open doors; in other fields it is the degree itself that counts or the degree and the school's reputation that counts. If the prestige of your advisor is not a major concern, it is usually best to avoid Professor I. Typically, Professor I sees himself as a consultant first and a professor second. Graduate students, except those who are teaching assistants who can cover his classes, usually have a low priority. As a consultant he usually has one area of interest, which makes him like Professor J; however, unlike Professor J he is rarely available. Because of his outstanding reputation in his field, he is also likely to be recruited in the middle of your dissertation by another university to booster that school's reputation. On the plus side, these busy professor/consultants may not be interested in dragging out the dissertation process.

In real life, a Professor I received low marks as an advisor. He was rarely available. When he was in his office he was always preparing for a presentation or finishing an article for publication. He would promise to review chapters on his trips but usually lost them. The student would come for an appointment only to find out that he had left town. In order to even register for dissertation credits the student had to meet the professor at the airport to get his signature. After two years and little progress the student changed advisors, topic, and committee and started over.

Researching the Pool of Advisors and Committee Members

Doing research on the individual members of the pool of potential advisors is essential. Unfortunately, that pool will be limited. In some cases the pool will consist of one candidate for advisor. However, your research will help you to (1) decide among alternatives, (2) develop the most productive relationships with the individual who becomes your advisor and the individuals who will become your committee members, and (3) help you select, narrow, or reject dissertation topics.

The Experience and Gossip Index

There are three main sources of information to explore. First is that of your own experience with the advisor/committee candidates. What kind of a relationship did you have with Professor X in class? Do you think she would rate you at the very least a good student? Was it a worthwhile class? Was he prepared? Was she reasonable? The "My Initial Impression of Potential Advisor Checklist" below can help you organize your data.

MY INITIAL IMPRESSION OF POTENTIAL ADVISOR CHECKLIST

Name of Candidate for Advisor: _____

Conclusion:

Advisor: Yes___ No___ Maybe___ Committee: Yes___ No___ Maybe___

	Low				High
How the candidate would rate me (past interactions)	1	2	3	4	5
Rating of candidate as a professor:					
(Class observation)					
a. Knowledge of subject	1	2	3	4	5
b. Class preparation	1	2	3	4	5
c. Timely return of papers	1	2	3	4	5
d. Interest in student ideas	1	2	3	4	5
e. Research interests in more than one area	1	2	3	4	5
Tenured member of department					5

31

Likelihood of staying two years (gossip)	1	2	3	4	5
Reputation in the department (gossip)	1	2	3	4	5
Reputation with other students (gossip)	1	2	3	4	5
Clues given that he/she may be interested in topics I have considered (articles, class, courses taught, grants)	1	2	3	4	5

Total _____

Comments: _____

_____

The Successful Dissertation Search

The second piece of your research will take place in the library. Schedule an entire day to review recent dissertations completed in your department (combine this research with topic research described in Chapter 3). It is amazing how many graduate students have never read any dissertations, much less the ones from their own department or those of potential advisors or committee members. People, including professors, tend to behave in a consistent manner. The dissertations they wrote and the dissertations they have sponsored will tell you a great deal about what you can expect your dissertation experience to be with a given advisor. Some of the data you will collect from reading dissertations will at least partially answer questions such as: What type of research do Professor X's students do, i.e., hypothesis testing or case studies? Are all of Professor X's student's studies related to a single topic? Are all the dissertations similar in format and presentation? How many pages do the dissertations have? What kinds of study populations were involved? Who were the committee members? Who were the students? The "Advisor Candidate Dissertation Research Check-

32

list" below was designed to help you organize your research findings (use the "Candidate Topic Worksheet" found in Chapter 3 to record potential topics you find during your search of dissertations).

ADVISOR CANDIDATE DISSERTATION RESEARCH CHECKLIST

Name of Advisor/Committee Candidate _____

Conclusion:
Advisor: Yes___ No___ Maybe___ Committee: Yes___ No___ Maybe___

Candidate Advisor's Dissertation:

Title _____

Experimental ____ Case Study ____ Other _____ Length _____

Dissertations Sponsored as Advisor or Committee Member:

1. Title _____

Advisor ____ Committee ____ Other Members of Committee Still on Staff _____
Name of Student _____ Date of Study _____
Length of Study _____ Study Population _____

2. Title _____

Advisor ____ Committee ____ Other Members of Committee Still on Staff _____
Name of Student _____ Date of Study _____
Length of Study _____ Study Population _____

3. Title _____

Advisor ____ Committee ____ Other Members of Committee Still on Staff _____
Name of Student _____ Study Population _____
Length of Study _____ Study Population _____

33

Ratings:

	Low									High

a. Number of dissertations their advisees have completed in the past three years

    1 2 3 4 5 6 7 8 9 10

b. Dissertations all or mostly on related topics:

   1. If you like the topic   3 4 5

   2. If you do not like the topic   1 2 0

c. Wide variety of topics   1   2   3   4   5

d. Usually works with the same committee and you have no known problem with any member   5

e. Works with a variety of committee members (based on your perception most weak/strong)   1   2   3   4   5

f. The shortest dissertation is:

   1. Over 300 pages   0

   2. Over 200 pages   1

   3. Over 100 pages   2

   4. Under 100 pages   10

                  Total   _____

Comments: _____

_____

The First-Hand Experience Search

    The third area of your Advisor/Committee research is done by interviewing students who have completed their dissertations,

34

those who have dropped or faded out, and those in the process. A word of caution here concerning students who have completed their degrees. There seems to be a euphoria syndrome that sets in when a student has graduated, making them see even the worst advisor through rose-colored glasses. Therefore, it is necessary to probe for specific information concerning their real dissertation experiences and not just to get a generalized rating. You want to know the answers to such questions as: Who selected the topic—advisor or student? Did the advisor help the student crystallize the proposal? How many changes were made in the proposal? Was the advisor available on a regular basis? How long did it take to get chapters back with reviews? How was the committee selected? Was it a helpful committee? How did the advisor work with the committee? Did any committee members present problems? How long did the entire dissertation process last? Would the person recommend Professor X as an advisor or committee member? Why? Another word of caution—the students you interview may have a continuing close-working relationship with the advisor/committee members you are considering, so don't share with them too much information concerning your motivations. Tell them that you are anxious to select a really effective advisor and would like their input. Don't tell them you are looking for an "easy mark" so that you can get through this stupid dissertation requirement as fast as possible. The "Experienced Student Checklist" below is designed to help you organize your research in this area.

EXPERIENCED STUDENT CHECKLIST

Name of Advisor/Committee Candidate: _____

Conclusion:

Advisor: Yes___ No___ Maybe___ Committee: Yes___ No___ Maybe___

Name of Experienced Student _____

Year Grad _____

Number of Months ____ Years ____ Working on Dissertation _____

35

Ratings:

	Low				High
a. Advisor and student decided on topic quickly	1	2	3	4	5
b. Once the design was set, the advisor did not suggest major design changes	1	2	3	4	5
c. The advisor provided effective input on statistical analysis or directed the student to good assistance	1	2	3	4	5
d. The advisor selected or helped to select good committee members	1	2	3	4	5
e. The advisor expected the student to finish the dissertation in a reasonable period of time	1	2	3	4	5
f. The advisor was available when needed	1	2	3	4	5
g. Drafts were returned quickly with appropriate comments	1	2	3	4	5
h. The advisor didn't change his/her mind once revisions had been made	1	2	3	4	5
i. There were no unexpected negative surprises at the defense	1	2	3	4	5

Total _____

Comments: _____

_____

_____

Selecting Your Advisor and Committee

It is now time to draw tentative conclusions from your advisor/committee research. It is very unlikely that any candidate for the position of advisor will have perfect scores. Some characteristic will have to be given priority over others. For example, the likelihood that a professor will be at the school until you complete your dissertation must be given high priority.

Some faults can be turned into assets or at least reduced in significance through planning. For example, take the case of the professor who meets most or all of the important criteria but is known to be leaving in nine months to accept an appointment at a prestigious university. It may be possible to convince her to take you on as an advisee and accept a tight time line, which will be somewhat of a guarantee that if you do your part you will finish in a short time. Other members of the committee will sign on with knowledge of your time line. However, this will only work if the professors involved feel a real responsibility to students once they have made a verbal commitment to them. At best a high-risk fault is like a high-risk pregnancy: the outcome may be worth it but even with the greatest of care there can be major problems along the way.

With priorities in mind, lay out your lists. Identify the best rated advisors for your situation. Some characteristics are negatives for everyone, i.e., the laissez-faire advisor. However, other characteristics may be pluses or minuses depending on your circumstances. For example, if the one-topic professor does studies of a population readily available to you, this can be a plus. However, if the particular population would be very difficult for you to study, then this professor and his topic may need to be eliminated from the candidate pool.

Narrow your advisor candidates down to two or three. Next to each list the pros and cons. List potential committee members for each advisor candidate, asterisk the ones who have been on committees with the advisor candidate in the past. Rank the candidate teams. Make a list of the implications for each team. Start with the advisor but note also implications for the committee. Such a list might include the following types of information and questions:

1. With Professor W, there don't seem to be any limitations on topic; however, most of the recent dissertations for which he

has been the advisor have been case studies. Do I really want to do a case study?

2. Students that Professor X has advised say he is a fanatic on literature searches. He wants every article ever written on every topic discussed. How is a hundred-page literature search going to affect my time line? Can I spend the required time in the library?

3. Professor Y has a reputation with past students as being very helpful. She is available and responds quickly to drafts.

4. Professor Z always seems to work with the same committee members. Are there any of these professors who could be real problems for me?

5. Etc. . . .

With your tentative lists, it is now time to consider potential topics. Your candidate lists will serve in most cases to narrow the potential topics and may set a specific direction. Before you make the final choice of advisor and approach someone to serve in that role, you should have a good idea about what topic you are interested in pursuing and what kind of study you want to do (see Chapter 3). When you approach an advisor, you want to strike a balance between presenting yourself as someone with a clear direction and someone who is open to the advisor's advice. You want to show Professor X that you have done your homework. For example, "I have read your recent research (book) on such and such, and also the studies Student A and B have done. I would like to do my dissertation on this topic, possibly using sample Y" (see Chapter 5).

When you approach a potential advisor, you also need to be prepared to discuss your time line. You want to be frank about your expectations of wanting to do the work in a limited time; however, you want to give the impression that you will meet the time line through hard work, ability, and discipline. You don't want to give the impression that the time line is more important than the quality of the research and that you just want to throw something together in order to get the degree. Explaining why you want to have a short time line can help put this in perspective. For example, I expect to be moving from the area in a year to a new position. The research experience and the degree (in that order) will be very helpful.

Be prepared for the possibility of rejection. Your assessment of the best department person to serve as advisor may match the assessments of a number of other students who got there first. The advisor you select may be unwilling or unable to take on any additional advisees. There is also the possibility that your research was inaccurate and the selected professor is not interested in your topic and recommends that you work with someone else. You may be able to use your persuasive powers to get the professor to change his mind; however, you may have to settle for your second choice.

Even if your advisor has been assigned by the department and therefore you have no choice, it is still important that you do an analysis of the pros and cons of the advisor. List the implications and plan your approach. If you are already working with an advisor, the process of going through the advisor review should help you plan for future interactions.

Care Instructions for Advisors and Committee Members

Remember that the dissertation is a rite of passage. You need to present yourself as someone making that transition. You need to communicate that you understand the professors' world, that you know that they have classes to teach, research to do, books to write, exams to grade, and other graduate students to advise. You want to strike a balance between self-sufficiency and dependence. You want to plan key interactions in ways that show that you are aware of their other obligations.

Keep in touch with your advisor; let him know that you are working. Share a little of the pain, "I have spent umpteen hours on identifying the right instrument for the study." Share a little of the joy, "I have really found it interesting considering the various ways I could collect the data. . . ." Balance keeping in touch against being a pest. Think of yourself as a colleague. What would you share and discuss with another professor? You also have to remember that you are still a student. For example,

39

if the norm is that students address advisors by their first names or if they ask you to call them by their first names, then do it. If the use of first names is not the norm, then don't. If it is within school, department, and the professor's norms, take your advisor to lunch while you discuss your progress. It is a balancing act between push versus pushy, and student versus colleague. It is a balance that should change over the course of the dissertation process. The change signals that the rite of passage is coming to a successful conclusion.

Summary

This chapter addressed the critical research work involved in the selection of the advisor and committee members. The roles and non-roles of the advisor and committee members in the dissertation process were addressed. The "Good Advisor/Committee Test" and profiles of good and poor advisors and committee members, with real-life examples, were presented. Specific procedures were discussed for identifying and analyzing your potential advisors and committee members and for working with ones already assigned. Finally, care instructions for advisors and committee members were suggested.

CHAPTER 3

SELECTING A DISSERTATION TOPIC

The "Right Topic" Selection Criteria—Forget Interesting, Go for Tolerably Non-Boring

Selecting a topic for a dissertation seems to be the biggest hurdle for most graduate students. One Ph.D. candidate was stuck at this point for fifteen years and spent a fortune on therapy before finally making his selection. If picking an appropriate topic is such a problem in completing the dissertation, then where do you start? Getting the matter into perspective is a first step. While topic selection is often the biggest hurdle, actually the specific topic of your dissertation is relatively unimportant. There are millions of acceptable dissertation topics in the world and probably a hundred of these would be acceptable for any given graduate student. Remember, the basic purpose of a dissertation is to demonstrate that you can do acceptable research in your field. It is not your life's work.

Selection of a topic should be guided by your goal of completing the dissertation. Specific criteria should be applied to determine the likelihood of each "candidate" topic's contribution to that goal. Specific criteria should include

1. Your knowledge of and experience in the specific area
2. Career advancement potential
3. Your access to the needed data
4. The time required to collect the needed data
5. The acceptability to advisor/committee

The Knowledge and/or Experience Criterion

Notice that the first criterion is knowledge, but not "interest," in a specific area. Surely, doing a dissertation in an area you find fascinating can potentially make the dissertation research more enjoyable; however, making the criterion for the topic "high interest" can also get you into impossible situations. For example, a student heard a researcher speak on brain research related to learning. He then read several interesting journal articles and decided that he wanted to do his dissertation in this area. However, he really had little knowledge of the field of interest; none of the professors in his department were working in this area; and as he narrowed the topic he discovered he had no access to the subjects he would need to study. Make your objective a topic that is "tolerably non-boring," a topic that has high potential for success (finishing).

Focus on what you know already. Make a list of topics on which you have already done research papers and taken courses. You may find that you have a considerable amount of work already done in terms of a literature search. Ideally, a graduate student would select a dissertation topic and know who their advisor would be early in the course-taking part of doctoral study. This super-organized student then would use assigned course papers as a means of doing preliminary work on the dissertation. In the real world this student is an extreme rarity.

Not all of your knowledge comes from graduate courses you have taken. What are the areas that you know about from experience? Are there areas of knowledge from your job that might be used as a base for a study?

The Career Advancement Criterion

The value of "future" knowledge should also be considered. Are there areas of study that may not only serve for the dissertation, but that can give you a leg-up on your career goals? For example, if you are a classroom teacher, but want to become an administrator, a dissertation related to administration may be more impressive to a potential employer than a study of classroom behavior of third grade students.

Ideally, your selected topic will build on previous research and experience and contribute to your beyond-the-degree goals. However, when it comes to final selection, *work already done* should probably be weighed more heavily than the potential value of uncharted territories.

The Access to the Data Criterion

Your ability to collect data needed for a study is another major consideration. One graduate student who had completed a number of papers related to the history of Cambodia decided to build on his acquired knowledge. However, his specific topic required that he collect data in Cambodia. Not only were distance and expense negative factors in his choice of topic but he waited years hoping to get a visa to enter the country so he could visit several temples, which were key parts of his study. Finally, he gave up and changed topics. This may be an extreme case; however, many students get into situations almost as difficult and a lot closer to home.

If you work directly with special education students, it may be easy to use them as subjects in a study of how they learn. You have access to their records, you plan their instruction, and you test their knowledge. However, if you require a large sample, you may need access to students in other schools and this may be a problem if you do not have *good* friends who teach in that field in other districts. If you are not directly involved as part of your job with special education, then it may be impossible to get access to special need students. Another example would be a graduate student who is working in a school district, but who wants to survey a large number of teachers. Unless you know some principals who owe you, it will be like pulling teeth to get them to try to convince the faculty to take time to complete questionnaires for some unknown graduate student. In other words, an ideal topic for one person may be an impossible topic for another, simply because of access. Access is so important that you should consider starting with identification of potential subjects and then back into a topic.

The Time and Collection of Data Criterion

Time is another factor related to your ability to collect data. How much time will it take to collect data concerning one subject? What is the minimum number of subjects a given study would require? How is the data to be collected? Can the collection be done on your time line? For example, a study requiring the thirty-minute group testing of fifty ten year olds can be done easily in one afternoon (assuming you can get access to two or three classes of students). But if your study requires individual testing of students, you may have real problems. First, it will take you a great deal of time to do the testing and this may be time you do not have, particularly if you are working. Second, you may have to collect data over such an extended period that questions may be raised by your committee concerning the comparability of the subjects. Third, individual testing takes more commitment on the part of districts. By law, regulation, or policy they may need to get parental permission in advance to allow you to do individual testing. However, remember: opportunity is the key—if your job is to test individual children, then a study involving individual testing may be perfect for you.

Studies requiring repeated measures can also be a problem. If you are doing a study concerning the impact on marsh land of the construction of nearby lagoons, you will need to take measurements prior to the dredging of the lagoons, wait for the dredging to take place (hope that the contractor doesn't run out of money and leave the project unfinished or have his permit tied up in court by an environmental group), and take measurements over time following the dredging. This is an example of a topic where a student may have knowledge and access but the time involvement is too great for a dissertation. This is a postgraduate study.

The Acceptability to Advisor/Committee Criterion

Acceptability of a topic to your advisor/committee is the last major factor. This aspect of topic selection was discussed in depth in Chapter 2. It suffices to say here that you need to weigh each potential topic against the interests of each potential advisor. If your advisor is known, then your topics are limited to those that will be acceptable to that individual. There can't be a shotgun wedding.

Remember that there are many potentially successful topics from which you will need to choose. The "Candidate Topic Worksheet" that follows is designed to help you organize your topic research and weigh the alternatives (a more comprehensive worksheet can be found in Chapter 5 for developing a topic into a proposal).

THE CANDIDATE TOPIC WORKSHEET

Topic _____

_____

Source _____

_____

Subjects used in original study _____

Potential study population _____

Papers completed on related topic _____

Courses taken related to topic _____

	Low				High
Knowledge of topic:					
a. From courses taken	1	2	3	4	5
b. From work experience	1	2	3	4	5
c. Interest and other sources	1	2	3	4	5
Ability to collect data:					
a. Access to subjects	1	2	3	4	5
b. Time required to collect data	1	2	3	4	5
c. Availability of existing data	1	2	3	4	5
Acceptability to advisor/committee:	1	2	3	4	5

Career advancement potential: 1   2   3   4   5

                        Total   _____

Notes: _____

_____

_____

To Experiment or Not to Experiment?

"I don't care what else I have to do, but I won't do a dissertation that uses statistics." This is a too common cry of graduate students as they begin consideration of a dissertation topic. If developing an appreciation of their subject is an objective in the minds of professors of statistics, then most are failing dismally. Students dread statistics almost as much as they dread the dissertation. Usually they avoid taking THE COURSE until the last minute, hoping that divine intervention will allow them to skip statistics. Having taken and passed THE COURSE, they then want to avoid any contact with the subject for life.

I would like to build the case for the experimental dissertation which uses statistics to test hypotheses. First, this type of empirically-based dissertation is clear-cut. You have one or more hypotheses, you collect your data, you apply a statistical test, you accept or reject your hypotheses, you write your conclusions and suggest how other graduate students could expand your work. An empirically-based dissertation is neat. Everyone (you, your advisor, your committee) knows in advance exactly what is expected. There is little room for committee-suggested *expansion* at a later date. Second, the experimental dissertation is usually shorter than other types of dissertations. Remember, experimental journal articles are short; however, they contain all the pieces required in an experimental dissertation. There is a limit on how much you can expand the written sections of a limited piece of research, even for a dissertation.

Third, you do not need to be a statistical whiz to do a dissertation requiring statistics. Whether you got an A+ or a C− in your statistics course, you are going to need professional help in

46

selecting the appropriate statistical tests and, most likely, in analyzing and interpreting the data. You are only going to be responsible for justifying the use of one or two statistical tests as they apply to your data. You will not be asked to demonstrate that you know how the formula was derived. Nor will your knowledge or lack of knowledge concerning the total field of statistics be called into question.

Fourth, the experimental dissertation with statistics used to test hypotheses may not be perfect, but like democracy, the alternatives are worse. Historical, philosophical, descriptive, and case study dissertations are usually messy. Expectations concerning the final product may not be understood by the candidate, advisor, and committee members in the same way. There is a tendency for them to drag on, as advisors and committee members suggest other avenues to explore or consider. Case studies are particularly prone to insidious expansion. Interviewing with the third set of subjects raises questions that should have been asked of the first two sets and requires additional data collection. It is difficult to draw conclusions and justify them with what amounts to a small sample. Advisors and committee members, while approving and sometimes encouraging the case study approach, often begin to ask statistical/experimental-type questions at the point where conclusions are being drawn. For example, "How can you conclude X, Y, and Z based on information from only five sites?" In the case study approach you usually collect tons of data and information, much of which probably will not match. For example, only one of your five cases has this characteristic, another case has a unique pattern of data, and two of your cases that are the most extreme in other ways are the same on some unusual characteristic. How do you pull all this data together and support your conclusions?

If you have a choice, the experimental dissertation has much going for it. If your major or your advisor (and you can't change advisors) requires that you do a different type of dissertation, then you will have to do additional and careful planning in order to keep everyone on task and moving along on a reasonable time line.

"Recommendations for Further Study"— A GOLD MINE of Topics

Okay, so you have considered the criteria for selecting a topic, but the bottom line is still finding a suitable topic that meets the criteria. The place to start is the university library. The typical library has hundreds of books listing topics with detailed supporting data on background research, subjects, data collection procedures, approved statistical tests, or other forms of analysis. The primary source is other people's dissertations. Virtually every dissertation has a section near the end called "Recommendations for Further Study" or "Implications for Further Research." This section of each dissertation suggests variations or extensions of the completed and approved study of a winner, a GRADUATE.

Is utilizing this source of a dissertation topic a form of cheating? The answer is absolutely not. A dissertation is an original piece of research, not an original topic. Important research findings are built up over time, each study adding incrementally to previous studies. A dissertation is a very limited study that should be part of a chain of studies that contributes knowledge to a much broader area. Dissertations that are unrelated to any other research in the field are less important in the long-range picture than those that attempt to add a small but significant piece to a larger puzzle. In some doctoral programs it is required that each doctoral student do research related to a large departmental study. One such student who was studying microbiology was given a list of acceptable dissertation topics at the same time that he was accepted into the program. The only question that he had to answer when he was ready to begin his dissertation was which topic of the topics still remaining on the list was the one he wanted to pursue. In another case, members of a group of graduate students were each given the opportunity to do a separate but related section of a major educational study. You probably have not been given a list of topics nor been offered a specific piece of a larger project; however, you can create those conditions for yourself by building on

48

any one of the dissertations already completed. The concept of building incrementally the knowledge base is also why departments or individual advisors guide or push students toward topics in certain areas. It is the way valuable research is done.

Strategies for Topic Mining

You can use at least three approaches to "mining" completed dissertations for topics. First, you can start with dissertations related to your strongest knowledge areas. For each topic you find, you can then consider what study population you would have the best access to and which topics would be acceptable to your potential advisor and committee. Second, you can start with dissertations that studied particular populations to which you have access. For each population you then consider your basic knowledge of the topic and the acceptability of each possible study to your potential advisor and committee. Finally, if you are a real pragmatist, you look for topics in dissertations recently completed in your department and by the students of potential advisors. You consider each topic in terms of access to study populations and your strongest knowledge suits.

Other Advantages to Dissertation-Mined Topics

The advantages of mining a topic out of completed dissertations go far beyond topic selection. Take the literature search, for example. A recently completed dissertation includes a complete search up to a given point in time. Filling in the most recent studies is easy. Your topic might deal with a different population or a variable not included in the original study; however, other dissertations can also assist you in identifying relevant studies in those areas. Acceptable approaches to stating hypotheses, size of study populations, how data were analyzed, and what kinds of conclusions can be drawn are all valuable lessons to be learned from *graduates'* dissertations.

49

Mining Accepted Journal Articles for Acceptable Topics

One of the standards commonly used for judging the quality of dissertation research is potential "acceptability" for publication in journals. The journals in the field are also good places to look for topics. Unlike the completed dissertations, they do not usually include specific recommendations for further study. However, it is not difficult to suggest how a given study might serve as a base for a different study population or how an additional variable might be studied.

The journal article is also a good model for the abstract and for the prospectus for the dissertation. It is relatively short but usually includes purpose, limitations, hypotheses, methods, results, and implications.

Using Your Current Career to Facilitate Your Dissertation

Another source of dissertation topics lies in your current employment. Doing research related to your current position usually carries with it that important plus of *access* to subjects. However, there are also other benefits. First and foremost, your research may be of real value to your employer. For example, in the public sector the agency may be receiving grant funds. Your research may provide the data needed for evaluation of the program. Because of the standards and the scope of a dissertation, the evaluation is going to be much more comprehensive than the usual program evaluation. The result of having such a quality evaluation may result in increased funding. At the least your work will be appreciated and you will have established yourself in a different capacity within the agency. You will interact in a different way with higher management and you will likely be involved with presenting your findings to the agency board. Your value to the organization will rise.

Considerable value beyond career advancement results from doing a dissertation on a topic of interest to your employer. It may be possible to work out an arrangement whereby you can collect data, spend time in the library, and do much of the writing on company time. In addition, you may have free clerical assistance, access to computer services, permission to purchase copies of related research, and even the services of other professionals.

One graduate student selected a research topic that was related to key issues in proposed legislation. The agency had such interest in the results of the study that it provided her with the services of all the professionals in a large department for three days. As a result, she was able to collect all the data from her sample within a week. Since the proposed legislation was to be enacted within a few months, another benefit was the justification of a short time line for doing the research and the dissertation. In general, the short time line is usually essential or at least very desirable if an employer really is going to get involved in your research project. Employers will see the value in their involvement in terms of policy decisions; the longer they have to wait for the information, the less their interest. If they have to make a critical decision or turn in a report for which they had counted on the results of your study and you miss the time line, your career quotient may take a nose dive.

Finally, employers who are interested in a particular piece of research may also be in a much better position to help you open doors for data collection in other agencies or companies. A letter from a graduate student seeking access usually does not rate very highly; however, a letter or a phone call from the top of one organization to the top of another organization usually gets results.

Advancing Your Career Potential Quotient by Selecting the Right Topic

If you are a full-time graduate student or if the very reason you are working on a doctorate is to get into a new career, then career potential should be a consideration in selecting a dissertation topic. If you know what you would like to do in the future in terms of a career, the dissertation may be an opportunity to kill two birds with one stone. Most companies and agencies have an interest in R&D that can advance their goals. Most companies and agencies have limited resources for R&D. Therefore, there may be real opportunity for a graduate student who wants to provide a "free" service. It is possible to enjoy all the benefits of the "dissertation related to current employer goals" listed above as an outsider to the organization. However, you will have to convince the organization that your work will be to its benefit and that there is no danger to the organization in cooperating. An organization can fire an employee who misuses information or causes personnel problems; however, the only control they have over an outsider is to stop access. There is another subtle or not so subtle control that should be pointed out. If this is the field you wish to enter and the organization you approach is a major actor in that field, then if you break its trust or don't perform, there is every likelihood that it will be capable of having a negative effect on your future career plans through the links organizations maintain. Even the most competitive organizations share a mutual contempt for disloyalty.

How do you find topics that may be of value to an organization and acceptable to your advisor? You need to do your homework on the current goals and projects of potential organization selections. What specific kinds of work do they do and with whom? What are their sources of income? Professors in particular fields may have in-depth knowledge of interesting organizations and personal contacts with them. People with whom you currently work may have worked for other organizations and have insights concerning how they operate and needs they may have. Once you have one or more suggestions for research, which would benefit a given organization, you need to lay out your proposal to someone high enough in the organization to make the decision or at least to recommend the decision to go ahead. A potential advisor may be the one to make the contact. The proposal you give the organization will not be in the form required by the university. The proposal should be brief and should show clearly how the research will be useful to the organization. You should also be prepared to write a separate report concerning your findings in a format appropriate for an evaluation or policy consideration. Even if you don't gain their cooperation, your "research on the needs" of specific organizations and your interviews with those higher in the organization will be a good basis for employment interviews later on. In some cases you may be told that the organization can't formally cooperate; however, they will be interested in your findings. This then provides an opportunity to go back with your completed work, the evidence of your value as a potential employee.

Selecting a Topic That Someone Else Wants Researched—Free Resources

A final place for seeking a topic is in someone else's back yard. Who or what institution does research in your area? Who may need you or at least tolerate you in order to get free help for a project in their interest? The most obvious source is your own department. Professors don't only teach: they do research. They do research because of (1) love of learning, (2) "publish or perish," or (3) grants requiring research or evaluation. Students frequently reject hints or suggestions from professors concerning topics. However, they are a terrific source. You get not only a topic but someone committed to that topic. Frequently, someone who has a deadline for results can become someone who has a real stake in your completing your degree. You may even produce a dissertation that contributes in a significant way to a set of research, a whole that is greater than the parts.

How do you tie into this source of a topic? You may need only to listen. If you already have an advisor, he/she may have suggested some areas to explore. If you don't have an advisor,

1. Pick a professor who rates high on the advisor rating scale.
2. Read what he/she has published.
3. Think how your access to subjects or job opportunities or knowledge might be used to extend that research.
4. Go see the professor.

Tell the professor that you have read his/her recent work and that

53

you are interested in doing research in that area. Have a suggestion of a topic or two, but really *listen* to the reply. The professor may suggest a different topic or a slightly different direction. If it is a do-able topic for you in terms of time and access, go with the suggestion. In this way, the professor will help you to define the topic and to set up the methodology. Your professor-with-topic search need not be limited to your university. If you are particularly interested in the research being done somewhere else by someone else, you may want to go to see that professor to explore how you could hook onto research in that area. However, remember that you will have to get a professor in your own school to be interested in the research of another university, so watch out for academic jealousy.

Another approach is to find out what grants have been given to your department or to other institutions that employ people in your field or that are involved with potential study populations. Grants may focus totally on research or may not involve research but require evaluation. The research grant usually comes with a set of topics and a limited budget. Free help from a graduate student is frequently well-received and can provide access to subjects and other resources. The grant requiring evaluation can also be an interesting source of topic. The recipients of these grants may not be interested in research at all; however, they have to evaluate the impact of their program. They may welcome with open arms someone who will help them with this task. The evaluation and the dissertation will have to be two separate documents; nevertheless, you will gain access to subjects and you may be able to get others to collect all your data. For example, a school district may receive a large grant for implementing an innovative approach to teaching basic skills to disadvantaged students. As an outsider doing research on a topic of interest to YOU, you would have little chance of getting access to students for testing. However, if you are doing what for them is the odious task of evaluation for their grant, it is likely that they will be only too happy to have the teachers collect the data, pay to have it scored, and pay for computer time for analysis.

54

Summary

This chapter addressed the selection of the dissertation topic. Criteria for selecting from the many topics available to each graduate student were presented. Concrete recommendations were made concerning the location of acceptable topics just waiting to be found. It was suggested that the topic research covered in this chapter be conducted in conjunction with the advisor/committee research covered in Chapter 2.

CHAPTER 4

SPENDING MONEY AND USING THE 20TH CENTURY TO YOUR ADVANTAGE

Dissertation Costs or the Longer It Takes, the More It Costs

Advanced degrees are expensive. Some of the costs, such as tuition and books, are up front and obvious. However, there are other real costs. There is the loss of income if you quit your job or take a sabbatical to attend class or to write your dissertation. Promotions or raises may be directly or indirectly related to completion of the degree; every semester of school can mean a reduction in potential income. Then there are the costs for travel to and from school, meals away from home, and maybe babysitters. In estimating the costs for your degree, don't forget the value of your own time—time preparing for class, traveling to class, and in class.

The dissertation can cost you a large hunk of cash. Universities require a minimum number of dissertation credits. Usually only one or two of these "courses" are actual courses that meet. Other courses are whatever work you do or do not do on your own or with your advisor. In addition, most schools require continuous enrollment in dissertation credit courses beyond the minimum, once you enter the dissertation stage. Some schools charge, in addition to course tuition, a hefty advisor fee for each semester you are in the dissertation process. If a semester goes by and you don't make any progress, you still pay. The longer it takes you to complete the dissertation, the higher the cost.

Figure out what your university fees will be for each semester you spend in the dissertation stage. Estimate your additional expenses, travel, lost or reduced pay, etc. How fast you get "IT" done is a function of your own planning, your topic, your committee, and how and when you spend your money. This chapter suggests ways to save both time and money.

PER SEMESTER COST WORKSHEET

Tuition	$	_____
Advisor Fee		_____
Travel for Appointments		_____
Travel to Seminar or Class		_____
Lost Wages		_____
Lost Salary Increases		_____
Other		_____
Total	$	_____
Semester Cost × Number of Semesters = Grand Total	$	_____

Word Processing, Form, and "Connie Comma"

You need to use word processing right from the proposal stage of your dissertation. This modern miracle can save you time and money. Corrections, additions, and subtractions can be made to drafts in minutes or hours and new copy submitted to your committee or advisor within days. No matter how carefully you prepare your proposal or draft dissertation chapters, your advisor and/or committee will have suggested changes. Suggesting changes is part of their job and part of the ritual. Inserting materials or making changes in traditionally typed copy requires either re-typing or results in messy-looking pages. Messy pages at any stage of the dissertation are a definite no-no! With word processing the changes can be made and the machine "re-types" and re-orders the pages, producing a pretty new copy. Pretty, easy to read copy discourages professors from suggesting further changes.

If (1) you have a good word processing PC and absolute letter-quality printer, (2) you are a good typist, and (3) you feel comfortable composing on the keyboard, then you may want to do your own typing. If two and three above describe your abilities, then this may be the time to buy a computer and daisy wheel or laser printer. If you feel more comfortable writing on yellow pads than composing at the keyboard, then you need to hire a word processing typist. While the typist is typing, or more accurately keyboarding, you can be working on another section of the dissertation. This is not the time to decide to learn to type or master word processing or to press into service a novice in this area, such as a spouse or friend, in order to save a few bucks.

Every university has at least one official or unofficial "Connie Comma." This is the person in the dissertation office or in your department who will determine if your manuscript meets the school's standards. This person will determine if your commas are in the right spots, what fonts are acceptable, what weight paper must be used, how the paper is to be bound, and when the document will be reviewed for compliance with all these standards. Even if your school has written guidelines and your advisor tells you not to worry about that "stuff" at the proposal stage, check it out yourself with the "horse's mouth."

Connie Comma can be a very good friend. Treat Connie with great respect. Frequently, this is the same person who will eventually schedule your oral and may be the person who decides if your manuscript is ready for the oral defense or who, after your committee congratulates you on your brilliant defense, decides if your dissertation is acceptable to the school and you are ready to graduate. Making an appointment at stage one takes little effort but can provide you with information that can save time and money later. If you are going to hire a typist, Connie can usually give you the names of typists who have frequently typed dissertations of successful candidates in your school. These individuals will know the format and, if they

59

have questions, will check back with Connie. In some cases it may even be possible to hire Connie as your typist.

If you can't get a lead on a word processing typist through the official university channels, try calling a few recent graduates for names of their typists. It is important that your typist be conveniently located. You do not want to spend a lot of time driving to and from with copy or to make changes. If you have to settle for an expert typist who has not completed recent dissertations for your school, buy two copies of the style manual, one for you and one for the typist. Have the typist prepare a couple of sample pages, which include footnotes and a sample reference page and get Connie Comma's stamp of approval. Hire someone who will assure you a quick turnaround time and who will be around for the next year. Finally, hire someone who uses an IBM-compatible or Macintosh computer and one of the very popular word processing programs. If the arrangement with your typist doesn't work out, you will want to be able quickly and easily to switch typists and give the new typist the already completed disks. Have your typists give you copies of backup disks every time changes are made or material is added. A few disks can move back and forth with the hard copy and you have a safety net.

If you have a word processor and compose at the keyboard, another possibility to consider is to type the drafts yourself and have the professional typist do the editing and formatting. This saves a lot of time. You don't have to worry about footnote formats, margins, etc., and your typist doesn't have to do the basic typing or try to figure out your handwriting. This method requires that you both have completely compatible equipment and software. Disks and copy are then just passed back and forth. If you are doing the entire typing and editing job yourself but don't have access to a quality printer, you may be able to use a printer at work to print copies of drafts and final copy. If you go this last route, be sure to use the printer at all stages; don't turn in material printed on a dot matrix printer that is too small or difficult to read, and don't plan to use a printer somewhere else that is hard to get to. Remember, a letter quality daisy wheel printer can be purchased for a few hundred dollars and time is money.

60

Finally, begin to use word processing at the proposal stage. Many pages from the proposal can be used in the final dissertation. Usually the tense has to be changed, from future to past, but this is easily done with word processing. No matter who does the typing, make two copies of every section and copy onto two separate disks as you complete a session at the keyboard. Keep one set of disks in a building other than the one where you are working on your dissertation. This is cheap insurance against catastrophic loss.

You Are a Researcher—Use the Phone, Hop a Plane

Remember the university descriptions of dissertations, in which the word scholarly was used? Start to think of yourself as a member of the scholarly community. Calling *other* scholars can save untold hours of library work and give you confidence concerning another dissertation requirement, "establishing credibility of sources."

Build into your budget long distance phone calls. A $100 phone bill can save you a whole semester in costs. It is amazing how helpful most of the top people in the various fields can be. Identify these people in your field, *read* at least their most recent article, then call them. Find out what they are currently working on that may relate to your topic. Get the names of other graduate students or professors who are working on related research. Check your understanding of how this scholar's theory or work differs from that of some other noted researchers in the field. Talking with practicing researchers saves time by getting immediately the most recent and relevant findings for inclusion in your literature search chapter. Such direct conversations can help you to further define your topic and/or methodology. It can also be extremely effective in the defense of your proposal and then of the dissertation itself. If asked a question on method or interpretation of another's research, you will be able to respond with, "I talked to Barbara Jones about that, and her view was. . . ." Finally, conversations with people who have devoted years of study to a field is down-

61

right interesting and can make dissertation research much more enjoyable.

Consider travel as an extension of the telephone. Sometimes while talking to a scholar you will be told about planned conferences or seminars that will focus on research very relevant to your dissertation topic. Such meetings will bring together several of the people whose work you will be using in your literature search. From your phone conversation with a particular researcher you may find that the department in that university or the professor has a library of related published and unpublished research that you can use. Hop on a plane, bus, or train or drive your car and go. Make a list of what you want to accomplish and who you want to see. Time can be conserved, dissertation quality increased, and, in the long run, money saved. You have spent thousands of dollars on this degree; don't quibble over a few hundred dollars more. Build into your trip budget funds to take the professor and/or others to lunch or dinner as a gesture of thanks for valuable information. Remember you are making valuable contacts in your field.

The Statistical Guru—A First Stop

Many dissertations will require the use of statistics. Unless statistics is your field, you need an expert. This is not the time to go to a friend who had one more course in statistics than you did. The time to get advice is when you have a statement of your problem, tentative hypotheses, and a description of the data that are available and that must be collected. Don't believe an advisor who tells you not to worry about the statistics until later in the process. Later, you may find out that you have a whole bunch of data collected that can't be analyzed statistically in order to accept or reject your hypotheses. So many graduate students hate statistics that postponing dealing with this important part of the dissertation ranks among the very highest reasons for failure to complete the degree.

Find the best statistician. The best is the person who is considered by your school or department as an expert. Statistics may seem like a straightforward field; however, there is frequently more than one *appropriate* test for a given piece of research, and advisors and departments may have preferences. The expert in your university may not agree with the expert in some other university or even in a different department or school in your university. The best is also the person who will take the time to understand your hypotheses, your proposed data collection, the characteristics of your data, and the characteristics of the population being studied. The best is also the person who will take all the time necessary to see that you understand how and why a test is used and what the results mean. Remember that you have to defend how you came to your conclusions.

Most schools or departments have professors who serve either as formal or informal advisors to students on research methodology and statistics. These people usually also advise other professors on their research and have high credibility with committees. If a committee knows that one of these individuals advised you on your methodology, it is unlikely that you will be questioned on this part of your dissertation beyond inquiries to make sure that you understand why and how this methodology was used.

University computer centers usually have people who will help you with statistics. These people are very skilled statisticians but are less likely to be familiar with applications in your field; therefore, you must be very clear in describing what you want to do and what data, in what form, you plan to collect. The computer center people may also be less known on an individual basis to your committee and therefore you may be required to defend your methodology more vigorously.

In most cases you will be able to get free advice on how data must be collected and organized and what statistical test to use. However, if you need lots of ongoing help and tutoring on why you are doing what you are doing, you may need to hire a person as a consultant. The initial expert you contacted may be willing to serve as a paid consultant or may recommend someone who can provide ongoing assistance. The initial expert is the one who should have name credibility with your committee; the tutoring or step-by-step consultant needs to be someone who understands exactly what the expert advises and can teach you to understand and implement the advice. (For a quick statistical reference see Chapter 5.)

Once your proposal has been accepted and your data collected, you have to complete the analysis. Universities usually provide graduate students free or paid computer time on their mainframe system. Unless you are very familiar with the computer center and system, you should hire someone to input your data and run your statistics and reports. The computer center can usually find someone, frequently another graduate student, to complete this largely mechanical task for you. Someone who does this kind of work all the time can accomplish this task quickly and, therefore, at very little cost to you. Once the data is run, check the findings with your statistical expert, to be sure it was done correctly and that your understanding of the results is correct. At this point, prior to writing the results and conclusion sections of your dissertation, some additional tutoring for in-depth understanding may be really worth the price. At this stage of the dissertation game you should also be working closely with your committee and advisor, and you need to know and have it evident that you know what your results are.

Microcomputers also offer interesting options for data analysis. If you only have a small amount of data, are experienced in using a PC, and have or can buy appropriate software, you may want to run your own analysis. Running your own data has at least two advantages: (1) you directly control the timing of the input and analysis, and (2) since you worked with the data and analysis you are more apt to understand the output. Statistical software packages are available for most PCs and are "user friendly." Unfortunately, the documentation for the statistical formulas is not usually very complete. For example, the documentation may not tell you if the level of significance is based on a one-tailed or two-tailed test for a given t-statistic. A good statistical software package only has to be good for your purpose; in other words, it must be able to handle your data and do the tests you need. Good doesn't necessarily mean expensive. One of the best I have used works on a Commodore 64 and costs less than thirty dollars. However, time and accuracy are the objectives, and these must be weighed carefully in deciding between hiring someone at the computer center to run your data and doing it yourself on a PC. If you run the data yourself, be sure to check the results with your expert on methodology and statistics.

To Quit, to Take a Leave, to Take a Sabbatical, to Work?

If you are in a situation where a fully paid sabbatical is available to you, this might be a route to consider. You will have six months or a year to leisurely do your dissertation and a lot of additional time to pursue other interests. The negatives to taking a sabbatical include (1) that you usually are committed to return to your old position for one or more years and (2) that the year that you are out-of-sight and maybe out-of-mind of your employer may not further your cause on the career ladder. If there is a residency requirement for your degree, you will probably need to use any available sabbatical time for that purpose. If you still want to consider a sabbatical, plan it for a time after you have your topic, your committee, and at least most of your proposal together. You can use the extended period of free time to collect data and write the dissertation. During the proposal stage, you need to visit the library, talk to other students, and explore advisors and committee membership; however, these are activities which can be fit into weekends, evenings, and a couple of vacation days. During the proposal stage there will probably be downtime while your advisor thinks about your proposed topic or is considering or contacting potential committee members, time while you wait for appointments, and the like. Sabbatical time is valuable; you don't want to sit around waiting until your proposal is approved, nor do you want to take a chance on moving too far into the dissertation itself without approval.

Most people do not have a sabbatical as an option. Therefore, they must decide whether to continue in full-time employment, get someone to support them for a period of time in the manner

65

in which they are accustomed, or quit and live in poverty. If you have a good job and that job provides a little flexibility concerning when vacation days can be taken, your best bet is to continue working. Working will give you the funds not only to support yourself but also to pay the bills related to the dissertation. The key to success is planning, not starving! Quitting your job adds tremendously to the cost of the degree. Such costs may never be made up through advancement.

Paid and Free Per-Diem Assistants

Another means for saving time and, therefore, money is to hire a per-diem or hourly assistant. This may require you to make a major change in your mind-set—that of the struggling graduate student; however, remember you are now in transition to fully certified professional colleague. Professors have graduate assistants, you can also have assistants. In your case, the assistant may be a high school kid you pay to run things back and forth to your typist or another graduate student you pay to enter your data at the computer center. Another valuable use of assistants is in collecting data. Suppose your dissertation requires collecting data from various sites around the state, such as demographic, test, questionnaire, or interview data. If you are working full- or part-time, it can be very difficult to collect this material. Your vacations may coincide with vacations of the subjects, and the sheer number of sites in your sample could extend the data collection phase over many months. The extended data collection time line may also raise questions concerning the comparability of data from various sites, i.e., teacher attitudes or student knowledge may differ significantly from fall to spring. Hire someone, train, test, and then have him/her collect the data. Or hire two or three people and get your data two or three times faster. In fact, all data might be collected in one day! You will have to test for inter-rater reliability for some kinds of data, i.e., interview data, but you will not have to defend changes that might have been the result of an extended response time. Be sure that you state clearly your plans for data collection in your proposal; some advisors may require that you collect at least part of the data yourself.

While it should be considered carefully, this may be the time to take your friends up on their offers of, "Let me know if there is anything I can do to help. I really mean it." This can be an effective means of collecting data or getting other forms of assistance. Work it out in advance; use them for really valuable activities (things that will save you time and money) and for very limited amounts of time, i.e., one day in the entire process. One graduate student, who picked a topic of interest to her employer, "borrowed" thirty willing co-workers for the equivalent of one work day. In one morning she trained them to conduct a required interview with subjects and tested their inter-rater reliability in collecting data. In the afternoon, the trained interviewers spread out over the state to thirty sites and collected all the required data for her dissertation.

Bartering for services should also be considered. Fellow graduate students may need access to data that you can assist in collecting without much effort, e.g., you work daily with the subjects of their study. In return for your assistance, they will help you with some meaningful activity. However, in the long run paying a stranger or several strangers may be the most efficient and reliable way to go, the way that will give you the most control of the end product and the assurance that friendships and relationships will be maintained.

As you prepare your proposal (see Chapter 5), make a list of all the activities that someone else could do (hiring someone to write your dissertation is not one of these activities); the required skill level of the assistance: whether it is available free, in exchange for services, or paid; and the dates of the needed services. Prepare and implement a plan for assistance.

Finding Someone to Pay You to Do Your Dissertation

There are thousands of public and private agencies and businesses that would benefit from research findings related to their activities. Most of these, particularly public and private agencies, have little in the way of funds to support research. What these groups frequently do have is an interest in solid information for decision making, access to data or subjects, and staff who could collect information as part of their jobs. In addition, they may have word processing services, excellent quality printers, computerized data bases, and data analysis capability.

The most valuable contribution these agencies or businesses may make to your dissertation is access to data or subjects. Subjects may not want to deal with an unknown graduate student, but may be happy to cooperate with a well-known agency or business that may be providing their funding or their profits. Another advantage of working cooperatively with a known agency or business is the opportunity it provides for career advancement. You learn a lot about the potential employer and they can get to know a lot about you. You will also be demonstrating your value.

If you think a business or agency can be helpful to your dissertation (or career), rewrite your proposal in brief form to show how the data will be of value to the target business or agency. Show them how your study will advance their goals or make their decisions more informed. Don't approach the business or agency through some low-level employee. It is the leadership that will see the potential of your study for policy decisions, who will direct others to give you access, and who may have long-term career value for you. Approach the leadership as a researcher doing a study that could be of benefit to them and incidentally to yourself, not as a poor graduate student in need of help. The leadership must be convinced that you can accomplish what you say you can in the time you say you can and that you will not cause them problems along the way. You will have to provide them with the results of your study in a format that is different from the dissertation format and on a shorter time line. Their interest will most likely be in results with policy implications. Policy research usually has a fixed time line by which decisions must be made and seeks answers to questions such as, "What do multiple sources of data suggest as the most viable alternative to select?" or "What is the most expedient or potentially effective direction to take?" If your data isn't there at the critical time, it may be considered useless.

Grants are also available for research if topics are carefully selected. However, writing a successful grant application may be as time-consuming as writing the dissertation. Another approach is to get a list of major grants that have already been awarded in your field of interest. You may luck out and find a local well-endowed grantee who is looking for someone to do the evaluation or research part of the grant-related activities. In addition, your university may have endowments to support grants for graduate students studying specific topics or in specific departments. Check these out.

Don't overlook the possibility of finding a topic of interest to your current employer. Your salary automatically is covered, and, in addition, you may get release time to write or collect data, as well as typing services, access to data, and, if your findings are really valuable, a promotion!

The Editor

You will need an editor for your proposal and for the dissertation. You get so close to your work that it is very difficult to catch technical things such as changes in tense or sentences that cannot be understood by anyone other than yourself. Committees are usually helpful in editing, but it makes a far better impression on committee members if even the most preliminary drafts pass the literacy test. An editor may be a close friend; however, this arrangement may lead to permanent alienation. Definitely hire someone as your editor if you are the sensitive type when it comes to your writing. The editor should know grammar, be really familiar with the dissertation style, be candid, and be skilled at working with technical writing. A creative-writing type is not the person you need. Dissertation writing must be clear, straightforward, and sometimes repetitive. It rarely contains adjectives and is almost always dull, dull, dull. You do not need an editor who is going to try to spice up your writing.

Remedial Action—When Your Advisor Moves or You Have to Move

Hopefully, you have picked an advisor or been assigned an advisor who is tenured and who will be at the university for years after you complete your dissertation. However, remembering Murphy's Law, it is not uncommon to find suddenly that your advisor has left your university for a distant school. In the case of one graduate student, the professor was deported to another country. Frequently, arrangements can be made for you to continue to work with the absent advisor, with a replacement advisor being added to your local committee. Such an arrangement can add a great deal of time to your planned time line. You need to develop a new strategy, not necessarily a new time line. Instead of scheduling meetings with your distant advisor, schedule phone calls. For example, before you mail a chapter, call your advisor to tell him that you are mailing, or better yet Federal Expressing, the chapter, and set a specific date to discuss the proposal by phone. Professors who have moved may have more interest in new assignments than in old graduate students. It may be necessary to schedule one or more trips to consult with your advisor. This action will impress the advisor that you are serious about finishing and adhering to your time line. Time is of the essence in this situation. The longer the time span, the more apt you are to find that your absent advisor has new priority interests and that your new advisor and your committee are less inclined to accept the directions your absent advisor gives you. This can lead to numerous rewrites or even the need to change or redefine your proposal.

The converse of the above situation is when you have to move. This may occur because you have completed your residency or assistantship and need to find employment away from the university. Career opportunities away from the university town or city may outweigh the disadvantages of staying in a job near the school. Don't become out-of-sight, out-of-mind. Confirm your dissertation time line with your committee, review your spending plan. Build into your plan specific trips to the university at specific stages of your work. Let your advisor and committee

70

know you are coming and specifically what you want to accomplish, e.g., to review the revisions to chapters 1–3, which were mailed to them on a specific date (or FAXed to them). You may need to reconsider the need for assistants. Don't decide that since you are starting a new job you will postpone the dissertation for a year—this is a sure way to become a member of the A.B.D. fraternity or sorority.

The Paid or Reliable Volunteer "Nudge"

Take a really honest look in the mirror. If you are a highly self-motivated and organized person, a "nudge" or "badger" is not needed. However, if you are in the least way a procrastinator, hiring a "motivator" or nudge is an essential investment. The badger is a person with whom you share your written time line and who promises to call and badger you on specific dates. It is necessary to find someone with the hide of a rhinoceros, who will not quit when given verbal abuse, or who will not accept your excuses. A close friend or "significant other" is usually not the person for this job. A mentor whom you admire may be an appropriate choice since you may want to please him or her to a degree greater than any postponement of a time line would allow. Your editor can also be a good candidate for this unpleasant job. If you pay someone for this job (if you are a real procrastinator, go this route), pay in advance and agree to pay double for any time line missed.

DISSERTATION BUDGET WORKSHEET

Word Processing	$ _____
Statistical Consultation	_____
Data Collection	_____
Data Entry	_____
Assistants	_____

71

Telephone _____

FAX _____

Travel _____

Tuition/Fees _____

Lost Wages _____

Nudge _____

Total $ _____

Summary

This chapter focused on the need to spend money during the dissertation process in order to save money in the long run. Base costs for your dissertation were calculated. Specific suggestions were made concerning budgeting expenses for physical preparation of the dissertation, work options, assistance, phone and travel connections, and "hiring" motivation.

CHAPTER 5

DESIGNING YOUR DISSERTATION AND PREPARING THE PROSPECTUS AND PROPOSAL

Designing the Dissertation

You have selected from your list of possible topics **THE TOPIC.** THE topic meets the criteria discussed in Chapter 3 better than other considered topics; namely, it is a subject for which the following are true:

1. You have knowledge of and/or experience in the specific area.
2. It will advance or at least not detract from your career goals.
3. You have access to the data needed for the study.
4. There are reasonable time requirements involved in collecting the data.
5. It is likely to be acceptable to your advisor/committee.

The next step in the process is really to define what you want to do in a clear and succinct form. This is your initial prospectus or proposal, which you will use to communicate your idea and plan of attack to your advisor and possibly to committee members. Developing this prospectus will clarify the who, what, when, and why of the dissertation for yourself. In addition to stating what you will do, it will make clear what you are *not* proposing to do. This is the short document that you will use to *test* the acceptability to your advisor of your topic and design. This is the stage at which modifications, enhancements, and limitations on the study will be negotiated.

The initial prospectus probably will not serve as the formal dissertation proposal required by your school. Most schools have very definite requirements for such a proposal. These requirements can range from a four- to nine-page description to the completion of the first two or three chapters of the dissertation.

73

DESIGNING YOUR DISSERTATION AND PREPARING THE PROSPECTUS AND PROPOSAL

In some schools the advisor is the only one who has to approve the formal proposal. At the other end of the spectrum, some schools require a formal oral defense of the proposal before the entire committee. The purpose of the initial prospectus is to get agreement on what you propose to do before the more intensive work of the formal proposal is begun. At this stage the focus is on just saying what it is you plan on doing, as clearly as possible, without concern for "dissertationese."

Are They Related or Are They Different, What Is the Question?

Now that you have a topic to propose, you have to decide what it is about this topic that you are and are NOT going to study. Dissertations ask and then answer one of two types of questions. Type-one questions ask how things are related. This is most obvious in empirical research studies. For example, "Is birth order related to future achievement?" However, type-one questions are also central to philosophical or historical dissertations, such as, "Were the writings of Peal influenced by his Southern roots?" In the empirical study of type-one questions, you use statistics that determine the correlation between things. In non-empirical type-one studies, information and argument are used to support conclusions.

Type-two questions ask how or if things are different. Again, type-two questions are most obvious in empirical studies. For example, "Is there a significant difference between students taught using Method A and those taught using Method B?" However, type-two questions also serve as the base for non-empirical studies. For example, "Were the factors underlying the revolt of 1888 different from the factors underlying the revolt of 1901?" In the empirical study you use a statistical test, such as the t-test as a basis for your conclusions. In the philosophical, historical, or literary dissertation, you use a variety of arguments to support your conclusions.

The first step, then, is to decide whether you will be asking if and how things are related or if and how things are different.

74

Write down the questions. Don't worry about the form or the exact wording at this point. Classify each question as type-one or type-two. It is possible to have both types of questions addressed in the same dissertation; however, it makes the dissertation more complicated.

What You're Not Going to Ask—Limiting the Study

What is it that you are not going to ask? In other words, what are the limitations on your study? This is a very, very important part of developing the proposal. Let's take a study that has as an initial question, "What is the effect (relationship) of dredging on saltwater marshes?" You need to limit the question for the purposes of the study. What is going to be meant by "effect," "dredging," and "saltwater marshes?" Effect may be limited to changes in the type of commercially valuable fish in the area. Dredging may be limited to that done for residential development. Saltwater marshes may be limited to one marsh area, e.g., in Barnegat Bay. The question then is rewritten to read, "What is the effect on commercially valuable fish of the dredging for residential development in one saltwater marsh area in upper Barnegat Bay?" The study is further narrowed through definitions, i.e., "commercially valuable fish" may be defined as those species of fish caught locally and sold through local or regional fish markets within the past year.

It is just as important to delimit the study questions in a non-empirical study. For example, take the general study question, "How are the psychological factors in Peal's life reflected in his writings?" Which psychological factors will be considered, which reflections and in which writings? The delimited question might become, "How were the psychological factors represented by Peal's childhood relationship with his father reflected as themes in his early fictional works written from 1910 to 1912?"

The exercise of delimiting the study question also assists in the development of sub-questions. For example, "What were the

75

psychological factors present in Peal's childhood?" "What were the major themes in his early works?"

It is better to over-delimit or narrow the study than to under-delimit it. Every limitation eliminates a piece of potential study and makes the work more manageable. Your advisor may feel that you have excluded an important aspect of a topic, but exclusions can be negotiated back in. Once you have had your proposal accepted, it is very hard to negotiate a factor out if you find that you have bitten off more than you can chew.

The General Design of the Study

Once you have your study questions clarified and limited, attention turns to selecting the general design of the study. How are you going to answer the questions? Are you going to pre- and post-test a group? Post-test two matched groups? Conduct case studies? Are there sub-groups that will be considered, i.e., girls versus boys, within two treatment groups? How are you going to ensure that your findings are the results of the treatment? Are you going to use each group as its own control, i.e., the same group gets both treatments at different times? Are you going to use a matched non-treatment group? There may be one overall design or there may be different designs for different sub-questions. It is important to be clear on the proposed research design at the prospectus stage. The basic design of the study will drive most of the work on the dissertation and will determine what conclusions you can reach. This is a basic element in the implied contract you have with your advisor/committee when they accept your proposal. You don't want them to say at a later date that they thought you were going to implement a different design. They may not accept your initial proposed design and it may be necessary to change some aspects, but, in the end, you want this part of the proposal really nailed down before you begin work on collecting data from your study population(s).

76

The What and How of Data Collection

Review of Completed Studies

What data will you need to collect to answer the research questions? Data or information collection are of two types. First, what have other people found out about each major element in your questions? In the examples given previously, these would include previous research on teaching Method A and Method B; in the study of Peal, research related to the effect of location on writers, major social influences in the South when Peal was young, and identification of his early works; in the saltwater marsh study, other such studies, environmental requirements for survival of certain species of fish, and possibly studies related to the type of dredging.

As in the section on developing questions, it is essential to narrow the scope of the data collection. When you go to the library, you should be able to determine quickly which studies are relevant to your work and which ones are not. This is where graduate students usually waste the most time. They spend an inordinate amount of time reading and taking notes on stuff that is not related to their specific research questions. If you don't already know who has done the most important research on each major element, you may want to begin by asking people who will know. For example, if your work is in curriculum and instruction and your study involves urban students, a lot of time may be saved by a short meeting with an urbanologist in the sociology department. If you have as a topic the extension of another study, your data collection may be limited to studies completed after the date of the base study. Even if you are not building on a specific completed dissertation, other dissertations may be very useful. You can take each element and identify a recent dissertation addressing that element, and the literature search will give you, usually in chronological order, information on major studies and major researchers.

At the prospectus stage, you want to identify the elements of interest and exclude those not relevant. Actual work in the

77

library should be limited to confirming that what you propose is do-able. For example, you may find that all of the completed studies related to one element of your study are so contradictory in terms of findings that you cannot use any of them as a base upon which to build a specific part of your study. You may want to revise your design to exclude this problematic element. After you have initial approval is the time to build neat small stacks of index cards or copies of studies, organized by element.

Collection of New Data

The second type of data that needs to be identified is the heart of your study. What will you collect from whom, under what conditions, using what method of collection, and when will you collect it? This part of the proposal needs to be very precise; both you and your advisor need to know exactly what you are going to do and NOT DO. For example, your subjects will be four whole heterogeneous classes of inner-city second grade students from one elementary school currently using Method C to teach math. Two of the classes will be taught math using Method A for one marking period and two classes will be taught using Method B for the same period of time. During the second marking period, the method used will be reversed for the classes. Each class will be taught by a different teacher who is trained in both methods. Achievement will be measured using the X Achievement test. Form U will be administered one week prior to the trial, Form Y will be administered on the last day of the first marking period, and Form Z will be administered on the last day of the second marking period. While children are heterogeneously assigned to classes, IQ, mobility, and the past years' standardized math scores will be analyzed to ensure comparability of groups.

While data collection may be the heart of your study, you do not want to collect a lot of data and then figure out what you are going to do with it. This is a common mistake, especially where survey instruments are to be used. It seems a good time to collect all sorts of interesting information as long as you are collecting; however, you will be expected to show the relevancy of all the information to your dissertation. This is a good way to get into trouble. For example, take our Method A versus Method B study: we can show comparability of groups with IQ, past achievement, and racial balance. But if you start to collect data on hand dominance, attitude toward school, and names of magazines in the home, you are going to have to explain the relevancy of each of these to achievement under Method A and Method B and any possible interactions. Keep it simple.

Instrumentation

Another aspect that must be decided upon at the prospectus stage is the instrumentation you will use to collect the data. When at all possible, use instruments that have been developed by someone else and that have been used previously in studies. Defending instruments you develop can be as time-consuming as doing the rest of the dissertation. If you fail to establish the reliability and validity of your own instruments, your data and results will be useless. There are thousands of tests for which reliability and validity have been established. If you use one of these, then you only have to argue the validity of the instrument for your study. You can find references to relevant tests in dissertations, research articles, test resource books, and in specialized test libraries such as the one maintained by Educational Testing Service, Princeton, New Jersey.

Existing Data

Some data you may not need to collect directly. Agency and government records may contain valuable data that can be used in your study. Some graduate students have successfully used only existing data from various agencies to answer their research questions. Not all departments will accept this type of study, and in most cases all the needed data are not available. However, existing data resources can be extremely valuable in establishing comparability of groups, identification of subjects, etc.

Why is it so important at the prospectus stage to identify how

79

and with what you will collect your data? The answer is that based on what you find available, you may want to change your research questions. For example, you may be interested in the development of high-order thinking skills, under Method A and Method B. Initially, you decide to use second grade students. However, you discover that the best test for your purpose has norms for grade four through ten. Therefore, you change your study group from grade two to grade five.

Defining the "Who" in Data Collection

Defining the "who" data will be collected from is also critical. In most cases you will be using a sample or samples; however, you will only be able to generalize your findings to the larger population from which the sample is drawn. If you use a study sample of inner-city kindergarten children, you will only be able to reach conclusions regarding inner-city kindergarten children, not all kindergarten children in the United States. If the inner-city children are all from one city, your conclusions will be further limited to generalizations about inner-city children in cities having children with similar characteristics. Whatever group you choose, you will have to show how they are representative of the specific population that is the focus of your study. This exercise of defining the study group leads in most cases to the "Recommendations for Further Study" section of the dissertation. Findings related to inner-city children lead to the suggestion that the study be replicated using suburban or rural children.

Data Collection in Non-Empirical Studies

In the case of a non-empirical study, information is still collected. In this case, the types of sources need to be identified. For example, in our Peal case, what sources are going to be used to identify the relevant social factors operating in Peal's childhood environment? Are interpretations of Peal's meanings going to be limited to those written in English? Are there particular identified themes that will be analyzed and others that will be excluded from the study?

Determining How You Will Get the Answers

Don't volunteer for unknown assignments. This is good advice for army recruits and also good advice for pragmatic seekers of dissertations. If you collect it, you will need to analyze it. At the prospectus stage you want your data collection and analysis to be lean and mean. It should go to the heart of your questions, provide the answers, and then get out. When you discuss your proposal with your advisor or potential advisor, you may end up adding one or more additional dimensions; however, don't volunteer at the start. Leave room for negotiation.

Getting the Answers—Decisions about Collecting Data

You need to know how and if you can analyze each type of data you plan to collect. It may be interesting and even potentially relevant to ask open-ended questions on a survey or test, but how are you going to analyze the information precisely enough to defend your conclusions? There are ways of handling such data; however, you need to determine the HOW before you contract to collect and analyze. For example, conclusions concerning the quality of writing can be defended on a basis of registered holistic scoring, holistic scoring, or T-units. There are many examples of the use of these techniques in research studies. Since the method of scoring determines the form and conditions of the data collection, instrumentation decisions (at least by type) have to be made at the prospectus stage.

Scoring or analyzing each type of data for each subject is step one. The next analysis question is, "How are you going to use the collective data to answer your research questions?" This gets you back to determining for each question whether you are asking if things are different or if they are related. In an empirical study, this means the use of statistics. Unless you are a statistical wizard, you are going to need advice in this area. Even if you were an A++ student in statistics, you are eventually going to want to confirm the adequacy of your planned analysis.

Analyzing Your Data—The Oversimplified Statistical Decision Guidelines

Obviously, a book of this nature cannot cover the field of statistics; however, the following oversimplified section may help you to get pointed in the right direction.

First, if you are asking how things are related, you are asking if things are correlated; therefore, you will be using correlation statistics. If you are asking if they are really different from each other (or more or less than something), then you will use tests of statistical difference. The next decision is whether to use parametric or non-parametric statistics. In general, if you are using data collection instruments that yield scaled scores or curve equivalent scores and you have a sample of twenty-five to thirty, you will probably use parametric statistics. If you are using survey instruments or tests you have developed or small samples (less than twenty-five to thirty), you will probably be using non-parametric tests. If you have a mixed bag—for example, standardized test but small samples—non-parametrics are probably the choice. Parametric and non-parametric statistics can provide the answers to your questions. The decision needs to be based on which statistical test you can defend. The following chart may get you started.

One note of caution here—while the field of statistics may appear to be cut and dried, in fact there are considerable differences even among experts as to which tests are most appropriate for which kinds of analysis. Departments frequently lean toward certain types of analysis. As you are reading dissertations from your department, see if there is a pattern to the analysis of data. For example, do most of the studies make use of multiple regression? This may mean that you should select research questions, instruments, and samples for which multiple regression analysis is appropriate. With such a department or with such an advisor, proposing a study using Chi Square is unlikely to be the best course of action.

THE OVERSIMPLIFIED STATISTICAL DECISION FORM

1. Sample Size: More than 25, Yes _____ Parametric _____

   Less than 25, Yes _____ Non-parametric _____

2. Type of Instrument: Standardized test, scaled scores, normal curve equivalents, Yes _____ Parametric _____

   Survey, self-developed tests, interviews, yes/no data, Yes _____ Non-parametric _____

4. If the answer to both 1 and 2 is "Parametric," select parametric test; if the answer to *either* 1 or 2 is "Non-parametric," select a non-parametric test. Parametric _____ Non-Parametric _____

5. Are you asking if things are related? Yes _____ Correlation _____

   Are you asking if things are different?
   Yes _____ Statistical difference _____

6. Based on your answers to 4 and 5, select possible tests. (Caution, remember this is only a partial list and there may be more appropriate tests for your data; over-reliance on this chart may be dangerous to your health.)

Parametric Tests

Correlations

_____ Single-variable correlation—test how one thing is related to one other thing.

_____ Multiple variable correlation (multiple regression)—tests how two or more things are related to one thing.

Statistical Difference

_____ *t*-Test related samples—tests if two related (i.e., pre/post) groups are different in some way.

_____ *t*-Test independent samples—tests whether two unrelated groups are different in some way.

_____ *F*-test—tests if more than two things are different (requires an additional test to determine which are different from which).

Non-Parametric

Correlation

_____ Spearman rank correlations—tests how two things are related.

_____ Kendall partial rank correlations—tests how two things are related while holding a third variable constant.

_____ Kendall coefficient of concordance—tests how more than two things are related.

Statistical Difference

_____ McNemar test—two related samples, "yes/no" or "before/after" type data.

_____ Wilcoxon test—ranked scores of matched pairs.

_____ Chi Square test for two independent samples—data falls into categories, "like/dislike," "change/don't change."

_____ Mann-Whitney U test—two independent groups, one group versus another group, in which scores can be ranked.

_____ Friedman two-way analysis of variance—three or more matched groups where data can be ranked.

_____ Kruskal-Wallis one-way analysis of variance—three or more independent samples where data can be ranked.

Note: When tests of correlation are used, it is necessary also to determine the significance of the correlation. In most cases in which a significant difference is found among three or more groups, it is necessary to find out which groups differ significantly from which specific other groups, using an additional test which looks at pairs from the groups.

Determining How Your Conclusions Will Be Drawn

Hypotheses

You have your questions, your tentative collection instruments, and your analysis plan. The final step is to clarify how you are going to reach your conclusions. In an empirical study the level of significance that will be accepted is usually set at $p = <.05$ (less than five chances in 100 that your conclusion is wrong). Your questions get turned into two types of hypotheses: (1) null, a statement that there is no difference or relationship and (2) directional, a prediction that there will be a difference or relationship and the direction of that relationship or difference, i.e., Method A will be better than Method B. Some advisors and/or departments want both types of hypotheses stated in the dissertation; others want only the directional hypotheses stated—again, let recent dissertations be your guide.

The Study Question and Sub-Questions

Sub-questions should line up neatly: one variable, one collection instrument, one statistical analysis, one standard of acceptance. The answer for your overall research question includes all of the results from your sub-questions. For example, one sub-question deals with the effect of teaching method on achievement in math, another deals with the effect on achievement in reading, and a third deals with the effect on higher-order thinking skills. The overall research question includes all of the parts and asks, "Which method of teaching results in highest achievement in basic skill and the development of higher-order thinking skills? What kind of conclusions will you be able to draw if you find higher basic skills achievement under Method A and higher development of thinking skills under Method B?" Your search of the literature on each element should prepare you for this possibility. You may find that previous studies of Method A, which take an incremental skill development approach to teaching math and reading, consistently show gains in lower level recall skill tests. You may find that previous studies under Method B have shown gains in thinking skills when tests designed for testing thinking skills in general were used, but not when standardized subject matter tests (which have few higher-order thinking questions) were used. Based on this information you may want to find reading and math tests that test content and levels of thinking skills.

Another approach is to anticipate the findings and predict (directional hypotheses) that teaching methods that focus on content skill development have a neutral or negative effect on thinking skill development, and, conversely, teaching methods that are content-free but focus on developing thinking skills do not have a positive effect on acquisition of specific content-related skills. This gets into the whole area of transfer of knowledge and the nature of learning. A careful review of the research related to your study should prepare you to predict the outcomes of your study; therefore, even though you have not collected your data, you should be able to anticipate your conclusions. Once you have thought through the likely conclusions, you are in a better position to finalize your questions, your data collection procedures, and your data analysis.

Why Do It?—Building the Rationale

Why did you pick this topic? What is it about other studies and findings that led you to propose a study on this aspect of the field, with this group of subjects? What is the small incremental piece that this study will add to the knowledge base of your field? This is the needs assessment part of the proposal. At this stage the fact that you selected the topic because your advisor suggested it or you have great access to subjects is irrelevant. Your job is to convince your advisor and committee of the need for this particular study. The development of the written rationale has been placed at the end, even though it will appear first in the proposal, because working through all the other parts will help you better understand what it is and is not that you are proposing to do. What you want in the rationale is a succinct and clear statement. Reading dissertation abstracts can be a useful exercise in preparing you to write this section.

The need for the study is established by showing that there is a problem of some importance, establishing that there is a gap in the knowledge base, and by showing why filling that particular gap is important or at least relevant. For example, let's look at a fictitious preschool study, using fictional data.

Preschool programs are expanding at a rate of 25% a year. It is predicted that by the year 2000, 85% of children ages three to five will be enrolled. It is also projected that there will be a severe shortage of college degree teachers for these programs (problem for society).

Two models of preschool delivery of services have received considerable attention in research studies. Method A uses college degree teachers exclusively for direct instruction of children. Method B uses the college degree teacher as the manager and non-degree senior citizens to deliver instruction. While each method has been found to be effective, only one study (Williams 1988) has compared the two methods under controlled conditions. The study found significant social development benefits under Method B. However, no attempt was made to compare the methods in terms of academic readiness (delimits the problem, relates it to existing knowledge and identifies the gap).

Development of academic readiness by direct teaching is a major part of current degree granting programs. If academic readiness is equally developed under both methods, then teachers in a degree preschool program may need training in instructional management and delivery of instruction through aides. Since there are more potential aides available for programs than degree teachers and teacher/aide programs are less costly, equality of the two programs would have social policy implications (importance of looking at this piece: teacher training and cost to society).

This study will compare the academic and social

87

readiness of preschool children who have participated for one year in Method A and Method B preschool programs at the time they enter public kindergarten (what it is that you propose to do).

The rationale should be understandable to any reasonably educated individual, not just to people in your field. The logic of your conclusion (the general statement of your study) should flow from the problem. An hour or so of reading and analyzing dissertation abstracts in the library should give you the hang of writing the rationale if you have problems with this section. One other caution: while you want to convince the committee that what you propose is suitable for a dissertation, you don't want to oversell the contribution to the field. In the example given above, it is not proposed that the study will solve the national preschool problem. It is suggested that the study could influence teacher training decisions and be of interest to policymakers because of costs. Also note that no matter which way the results come out, the value of this study could be defended. This is an important consideration when designing a study.

Preparing the Initial Proposal Prospectus

The initial prospectus stage is where the most critical work is done. This is where the implied contract between you and your advisor/committee is negotiated. Once you complete this stage, the work of the dissertation in terms of difficulty is downhill. However, first you need to move from the point where you have a topic, questions, design, etc., to the "signed contract point." There is considerable variance among schools, within schools, and among advisors on how this step should be accomplished. The official process for the proposal may actually be to write and submit the first three chapters. However, you don't want to spend all that energy and time on an idea or approach that will not be accepted; therefore, an initial prospectus is developed. The form or outline presented below is designed to help you clarify in your own mind the what, when, how, and why of the study.

88

INITIAL DISSERTATION PROSPECTUS FORM

Topic: _____

_____

Research Question

_____

_____

_____?

Does it ask how things are related (yes ____ no ____) or
different (yes ____ no ____)?

Limitations

Element/Variable   Limitations

1. _____   A. _____
                              B. _____
                              C. _____

2. _____   A. _____
                              B. _____
                              C. _____

3. _____   A. _____
                              B. _____
                              C. _____

Sub-Questions

1. _____

_____

89

2. _____

_____

3. _____

_____

General Design of Study

_____

_____

_____

Related Studies

Element/Variable   **Most Important Studies**

1. _____   A. _____
                             B. _____
                             C. _____

2. _____   A. _____
                             B. _____
                             C. _____

3. _____   A. _____
                             B. _____
                             C. _____

Combination Studies

A. _____   B. _____

C. _____   D. _____

E. _____   F. _____

Study Population

Characteristics of Population

1. _____   2. _____

3. _____   4. _____

Selection of Sample/Control _____

_____

_____

Size of Sample _____ Size of Control _____

Available Related Data

Type of Data	Source
1. _____	_____
2. _____	_____
3. _____	_____

Data to Be Collected for Study

Question #	Instrument(s)	Analysis Parametric/ Non- Parametric	Stat. Test
1. _____	_____	_____	_____
2. _____	_____	_____	_____
3. _____	_____	_____	_____

Directional Hypotheses	Anticipated Conclusions
1. _____	_____
_____	_____

2. _____   _____

   _____   _____

3. _____   _____

   _____   _____

Rationale for Study

The Big Problem _____

_____

_____

What Is Known _____

_____

_____

_____

The Gap _____

_____

The Study _____

_____

_____

_____

Working Title _____

_____

_____

The Proposal Format

The format suggested above as a means of initially organizing the information would be inappropriate for a prospectus submission. What format would be appropriate? This is where your previous research on advisors, collected from current and past graduate students, comes into play. The appropriate format for the prospectus should be matched to your knowledge of your advisor or potential advisor. The process may have several steps. For example, if you know who your advisor is and she has suggested the area of study you are proposing, then your proposal might be a couple of pages on proposed method. In this case you can assume that the advisor knows the importance of the study. The description of the methods and verbal exchange with the advisor serves to set the parameters. This may lead to development of a *second* more detailed four- to nine-page prospectus that the advisor or candidate would share with potential committee members.

In the case where the advisor is not a definite known, the first step may be a four- to nine-page summary of what is proposed. The target advisor may want to base the decision concerning becoming the advisor for the study on a written prospectus that will allow him to judge how much thought has gone into the study idea, how much work as an advisor the study is likely to take, and how committed the student is to completing the degree. Even if you know your advisor, but you have been at the "initial prospectus" stage for some time, the more complete written proposal may be the way needed to signal the advisor that you have stopped fooling around and are really serious about doing a study and finishing the degree.

The four- to nine-page summary can be taken from the "Initial Dissertation Proposal Form"; however, the order of presentation is different and it is in narrative form. The finished document should look a lot like the required dissertation summary that eventually you will submit with your dissertation for inclusion in *Dissertation Abstracts International*; what is left out is the summary of actual results and conclusions. The following outline may be helpful as a guide.

PROPOSAL OUTLINE

I. Rationale for the Study

   A. The big problem

    B. What is known
    C. The gap
    D. General study problem statement

II. Research Questions

    A. The overall directional research hypothesis
    B. Sub-questions and/or sub-directional hypotheses
    C. Limitations
    D. Key definitions

III. Methods and Procedures

    A. General design of study
    B. Study population and sample selection
    C. Data collection instruments
    D. Data collection procedures
    E. Analysis procedures

Planning the Advisor/Advisee Proposal Interaction

Remember that this is the proposal stage of the dissertation. What you propose is wide open for negotiation. Don't expect your advisor or potential advisor to hear or read your proposal, pat you on the head, and tell you to go for it. Hopefully, you will get approval of the basic thrust of the study and the methodology; however, expect suggestions for modifications. This is not the time to dig in your heels and become defensive about your work. Listen to suggestions and counterproposals. Advisors ARE ADVISORS and they can be most helpful at this stage. If some of the suggestions seem unreasonable, you may be able to negotiate around them, but be prepared to EMBRACE some of their suggestions, include them in your final proposal, and say thank you. If the suggestions become requirements and you don't think you can live with them, then you may need to prepare a different proposal for possibly a different advisor. If you have done your homework on advisors and completed dissertations in your department and have taken a pragmatic approach

94

to developing the proposal, you should not find yourself in the position of needing to start over with a different proposal.

One last caution—sometimes you think you have really lucked out. The advisor reads your initial prospectus, listens to your description of the study and says, "Go ahead and develop the final proposal." This is the time to probe a little before you rush off to start writing. They really may be saying, "You have a good start, write it all up, and then the committee and I will make suggestions." Time can be saved later by encouraging some more discussion of specific aspects of the proposal. For example, "Do you think the sample of thirty students will be considered large enough?"

This is also the time to start to talk about other potential committee members, a time to suggest possible members based on your research and on your topic. Your objective is to identify the members, get them to agree to serve, and get their input concerning the initial proposal. In some schools you will be expected to approach potential committee members and ask them to serve; in other schools your advisor will approach potential committee members. In some schools the advisor will "mention your interest" to a potential member and then you will set up an appointment to ask them to serve.

The initial prospectus should have attached to it your proposed time line for completing the dissertation and graduating. This is important for several reasons. First, it forces you to make a commitment of a date to emerge from the tunnel. Second, it signals the advisor that you are serious and that time spent with you will not be wasted. Third, it provides the advisor and potential committee members with information that may affect their decision to serve. Professors have their own set of time lines. They may be working on a large study with deadlines, be planning a sabbatical, have many other doctoral students they are advising, or be planning to retire or leave the university. Your time line may or may not fit with their needs or plans. You need to find this out up front.

The initial prospectus may or may not get developed into a much longer proposal. It may actually become chapters of the dissertation or you may just be required to modify or expand slightly your initial work. The formal acceptance process of the final proposal can take several forms. The advisor may be the only one who signs off on the proposal, or at the other extreme there may be an oral defense of the first three chapters of the dissertation before the entire committee and any member of the department including other graduate students. Obviously, the former, advisor-only, is the easiest at this stage; however, there is a real advantage to a process that has the entire committee sign off on the proposal. The more formal the approval process is, the more like a fixed contract the proposal becomes. If you hold up your end of the contract, then it is very unlikely that there will be major changes later on in the process.

Summary

This chapter dealt with the step-by-step process of designing the dissertation and preparing the proposal. Definition of the research question, limiting the study, data collection and analysis, and development of the rationale were covered in detail. Both empirical and non-empirical studies were considered; however, a pitch was made in support of the empirical study as being easier to complete successfully. Finally, the development of the INITIAL PROSPECTUS and THE PROPOSAL were discussed.

======= CHAPTER 6 =======

WRITING THE DISSERTATION—TWENTY WORKDAYS TO GO!

Getting Organized for the Final Push

With your proposal accepted, it is a downhill run to the end of the course. At the rate of only one page an hour, you can write the actual dissertation in less than three work-weeks. Figure another week for revisions and *voila*, the end is in sight.

Now is the time to get organized for the final push. Most things are easier to do if you have a model or set of directions or if you have done them before. The dissertation is unique in that it is something you do only once. Your department may provide a document explaining what the cover format should be, the paper quality and print fonts required, format for footnotes and acceptable style manuals. However, in most cases little else is provided. The style manuals provide excruciatingly detailed information on the minutiae of format, i.e., indentation, hierarchy of headings, footnotes, abbreviations, and bibliographic references.

Faced with 50 to 100 blank pages that will become your dissertation, style manuals and university outlines are not very helpful in getting you organized and started. It is time to return to the "textbook of completed dissertations" for a plan of action. Revisit the dissertations you reviewed in searching for a topic, preparing a proposal, and researching your committee. You want to find dissertations with as many of the following characteristics as possible:

1. Short, preferably under 100 pages
2. Recently accepted by your advisor
3. Similar in design to your study
4. A logical set of headings
5. Similar in topic to your study

The next step is to dissect dissertations to determine their exact anatomies. You want to identify the chapters, subheadings, number of pages, and number of paragraphs. Following are two examples, from two different universities, of dissertation anatomy analyses.

EXAMPLE 1: CORRELATION ANALYSIS STUDY

Chapters and Subheads		# of Pages	# of Paragraphs
I. INTRODUCTION			
Background		3.25	9
Statement of the Problem		.5	1
Definitions		4.5	19
Limitations		.75	3
Significance		.75	2
	Subtotal	9.75	34
II. REVIEW OF THE LITERATURE			
Introduction (summary)		.75	3
Competency Standards		6.0	15
Socioeconomic Status		5.0	9
Quality of School Services		8.5	15
Politics and Evaluation		5.0	19
Rationale and Hypotheses		8.0	19
	Subtotal	33.25	80
III. PROCEDURES AND METHODOLOGY			
Introduction (summary)		.25	1
Population		.5	1
Data Collection and Treatment			
Introduction		.25	1
Local Standard Data		1.75	9
State Standard Data		.75	2
District Factor Grouping Data		.75	3
Statistical Treatment		3.25	6
	Subtotal	7.5	23

Chapters and Subheads	# of Pages	# of Paragraphs
IV. PRESENTATION AND ANALYSIS OF DATA		
Introduction (summary)	1.0	2
Testing the Hypotheses	19.0*	36
Subtotal	20.0	38
V. DISCUSSION AND CONCLUSIONS		
Introduction (summary I–III)	1.0	1
Summary of Findings	4.0	8
Discussion of Findings	6.5	12
Integration and Implication of Findings	1.0	1
Recommendations for Further Study	2.0	4
Subtotal	14.5	26
TOTAL	85	201
APPENDIX	6	
SELECTED BIBLIOGRAPHY	3	

*Excludes 7 pages of charts.

EXAMPLE 2: MARSH AND DREDGING STUDY

Chapters and Subheads	# of Pages	# of Paragraphs
I. PROBLEM AND INTRODUCTION		
Introduction	1.0	3
Problem	.5	1
Hypotheses	1.0	4
Subtotal	2.5	8
II. REVIEW OF RELATED RESEARCH		
Water Quality Research	8.0	25
The New Jersey Case	.75	2
Dredging and Filling Effects	6.0	20
Subtotal	14.75	47

Chapters and Subheads		# of Pages	# of Paragraphs
III. METHODS AND MATERIALS			
Operational Definitions		.5	3
Assumptions and Delimitations		1.0	5
Description of Study Area		5.0	16
Data Collection		7.0	33
Statistical Analysis		2.0	8
	Subtotal	15.5	65
IV. RESULTS			
Physical Parameters		3.5	9
Biological Parameters		6.0	19
Ecological Parameters		2.0	5
	Subtotal	11.5*	33
V. CONCLUSIONS, GENERALIZATIONS, IMPLICATIONS, AND SUGGESTIONS			
Conclusions		5.0	19
Generalizations		3.0	9
Implications		2.5	5
Suggestions for Further Study		1.0	4
	Subtotal	11.5	37
	TOTAL	55.75	190
APPENDICES		40	
REFERENCES		5	

*Excludes 15 pages of charts, maps, and diagrams.

Take a couple of dissertations that most closely meet the criteria listed above and do an analysis of each. It only takes fifteen to twenty minutes to dissect each one in this manner, and it will give you a real feel for the project. Forget the content of the dissertations, focus on the structure. For example, note that while the chapter headings are probably quite similar, the subheads vary considerably. You may find that the hypotheses in one study are listed in the first chapter and in another study in the second chapter. Dissertations done in some schools may have a one or two paragraph summary of what is contained in the chapter as an introduction to chapters 2–4 and a summary of chapters 1–4 as an introduction to chapter 5. In two dissertations of approximately the same length, you will probably find considerable differences in the length of particular chapters. Note also the length and type of information contained in the appendices. A lot of dissertations that look thick contain appendices that have more pages than the dissertation proper. This is not unusual. Copies of instruments, item-by-item survey results, certain computer analyses, profiles of subjects, and even some correspondence can be appropriately found in appendices.

The purpose of analyzing the anatomy of dissertations is to prepare you to develop the anatomy for your own dissertation. The idea is to determine in advance all the headings, the number of pages for each section, the number of paragraphs for each section, and the total length of your dissertation. You build your model based on completed (successful) dissertations. You may not find one dissertation that meets all five of the criteria. It may be necessary to develop a combination structure. Note that "similar topic" is listed fifth among the criteria. Format is what you are after at this point. You may find a methods chapter in one dissertation, which parallels your methodology (the topic may be entirely different), which you will use as the model (subheads, number of pages, number of paragraphs, writing style). In another dissertation a parallel literature search is clearly and succinctly presented. This literature search becomes the model for your own literature search. Later, dissertations on the same or similar topics can be useful as models for presenting content. Dissertations on the exact topic may actually present a danger when used as models; it may be difficult to avoid plagiarizing the actual writing. At this point characteristics 1 through 4 are the most important—"short," "advisor-accepted," "design," and "a logical set of headings." The other piece that you need at this time is your proposal. Armed with your proposal and one or more "model" dissertations, you are ready to develop the skeletal structure of your own dissertation. The following form can help you analyze other dissertations and develop the anatomy of your dissertation.

DISSERTATION OUTLINE

Chapter	# of Pages	# of Paragraphs
I. _____ (Introduction, Problem, Purpose)		
A. _____	_____	_____
B. _____	_____	_____
C. _____	_____	_____
D. _____	_____	_____
E. _____	_____	_____
II. _____ (Related Literature)		
A. _____	_____	_____
B. _____	_____	_____
C. _____	_____	_____
D. _____	_____	_____
E. _____	_____	_____
F. _____	_____	_____
III. _____ (Methods and Procedures)		
A. _____	_____	_____
B. _____	_____	_____
C. _____	_____	_____
D. _____	_____	_____
E. _____	_____	_____
IV. _____ (Results)		
A. _____	_____	_____
B. _____	_____	_____
C. _____	_____	_____

Chapter	# of Pages	# of Paragraphs
D. _____	_____	_____
E. _____	_____	_____
V. _____	(Discussion, Conclusions, Implications, Further Study)	
A. _____	_____	_____
B. _____	_____	_____
C. _____	_____	_____
D. _____	_____	_____
E. _____	_____	_____
Appendices		
A. _____	_____	_____
B. _____	_____	_____
C. _____	_____	_____
References	_____	

Planning the Final Attack—You Can Do More Than One Thing at a Time

Armed with your detailed skeletal outline and having determined the exact number of pages and paragraphs in your dissertation and your accepted proposal, you are ready to develop the attack plan. Developing the work plan may be your LONGEST WORKDAY, but it is worth the effort. This is another point where graduate students clutch or have a panic attack. To sit down with a blank page or screen and insert the number 1 is to invite paralysis. Your proposal already has some version of a page one (and probably a two and three, etc.). Later (much later), or as the very last thing you do, you will review and pos-

WRITING THE DISSERTATION—TWENTY WORKDAYS TO GO!

sibly modify these introductory pages, but not now. The task now is to PLAN. Remember, the approach to writing a dissertation presented in this book is pragmatic. Your plan needs to maximize your efficiency and ensure that you reach your time deadline.

Step one is the development of lists. Identify the major activities and use them as headings, each on a separate piece of lined paper. Each of your headings will represent a set of activities. Assign a letter to each list. Headings might include: (A) Literature search topic #1 _____ , (B) Literature search topic #2 _____ , (C) Finalize sample, (D) Selection of final set of instruments, (E) Data collection, (F) Finalize statistical treatment, (G) Complete analysis of data, (H) Population description. In some cases a particular heading might have two or three discrete sets of activities; treat each to a separate list. Start with any one of the topics. Write in the "list letter," "topic," "chapter #," and "subhead." Now list ALL the steps that you must take to get to the point where you can write the section. Next to each item, place a tentative completion date and the estimated amount of time actually to do the activity. For example, it may take two weeks to get responses from a letter requesting permission to interview children; however, it will only take you thirty minutes to write the letter, one hour to address the envelopes and mail them, and three hours to make phone calls to those that don't respond in writing. A sample work list might well look like this:

SAMPLE WORK LIST

List: C

Topic/Activity: Finalize Sample Section

Insert Chapter: 2   *Subhead:* Description of Sample   *Appendix:* B

	Hours	Date	Done
Write Section: # pages 1 # paragraphs 4	1	12/7	_____
1. Call John in sample school for current enrollment list	.25	11/11	_____

	Hours	Date	Done
2. Call Harry in control school for current enrollment list	.25	11/11	_____
3. Write parent letter to sample students for permission to interview	.30	11/10	_____
4. Get signed letter from John	.00	11/18	_____
5. Get a table of random numbers	.15	11/14	_____
6. Select sample from list +20%	.15	11/16	_____
7. Select control from list +20%	.15	11/16	_____
8. Finalize date with paid graduate student to go to the two schools to record test data	.20	11/11	_____
9. Confirm date with John and Harry	.00	11/11	_____
10. Make up a sheet for recording data to be collected by graduate student	.15	11/16	_____
11. Send letters to parents	1.00	11/19	_____
12. Conduct follow-up phone calls to non-respondents	3.00	11/28	_____
13. Finalize sample and control lists based on completed data lists	.30	12/1	_____
14. Using letters instead of names make two charts showing student, scores, IQ, and total number in sample and control	1.00	12/1	_____
15. Have charts typed in final form as Appendix B by typist	.05	12/2	_____
16. Grad student goes to sites to record test, IQ, address, telephone number, and date of birth for each student on the list (half-day each site)	.00	11/18	_____

As you develop and check each list, you will discover that you think of items that, in terms of time, should appear earlier on the list. Don't bother to redo the list (don't be compulsive about neatness), the date will determine the order. Notice in the above example activities to be done by the person writing the dissertation are grouped. The idea is to handle a particular section as few times as possible. For example, Monday, November 11th, phone calls are placed to Harry, John, and to the to-be-employed-by-you graduate student. The calls to John and Harry not only ask for the list but confirm the date of your employee's visit, and John is told that the parent letter is in the mail and that your staff member will pick it up on 11/18. Notice also that work done by others is projected as zero time; list times relate to your work only. In this example, writing activities are planned for weekends, phone calls to parents during business hours or evenings. Finally, as projects are finished, the need is to get them really finished, i.e., send the Appendix B for final typing. The work goes much more quickly if you do all the things related to a set of activities while you are focused on those activities, i.e., write the letter and make up the recording sheet. In reviewing your plan, mark items that, in terms of time, are essential. For example, it is important that your employee collects the data on the planned date. If he postpones the visit, you will have to rearrange the visit and you will not be able to write the section on 12/7. You need to build contingency plans around essential activities and dates; i.e., if your graduate student calls to postpone, then you will take an emergency vacation day from work and do it yourself.

Putting Your Plan Together

You have sliced and diced the dissertation into its smallest pieces. It is now time to put the work plan together in time sequence. You want to take the activities from the individual lists and re-order the activities into a weekly schedule that ends with graduation week. At this stage you will also identify the constraints, i.e., activity 2 from list A (2A) must be done before activity 1 from list C (1C) can be done; Chapter II must be submitted to Advisor X by 12/10 or he will not be able to respond until he returns from Paris three weeks later! The technique for laying out the plan is a variation on PERT (Program Evaluation Review Technique), a technique widely used by the Department of Defense in research and development projects. The similarities between writing a dissertation and the development of a weapon system are obvious (Cook 1979).

Your Week Line

Take eight to ten sections of fan-fold computer paper or a roll of shelf paper. From top to bottom draw lines, about four inches apart, one for each week, from now till graduation. Write the date of each consecutive Monday at the top of each line.

SAMPLE WEEK LINE

Nov.	Nov.	Nov.	Nov.
4	11	18	25

Your Major Events with Dates

The next activity is to make your plan come out right by identifying major events. What must you do in order to graduate on time? At the far right hand of the chart, draw a box in ink in the week column of graduation, label it "Graduate," and put in the exact date. Move to the left and draw a box for the last day you can submit the edited, revised, final copies of the dissertation to the dissertation office in order to graduate: label it "Sub. to

107

Diss. Office." Move to the left and place a box in the week of your defense, label it "Defense," and put in the exact date. Move to the left and draw a box: label it "Final to Committee" with the date. Continue moving to the left and draw boxes (switch to pencil, you may have to move these boxes as you add the other activities) to represent when each chapter will be submitted to your advisor and committee. When you have all the boxes, connect them with dotted lines, except for the last two boxes on the right. Connect these two boxes with a solid line, since there is no work to be done between the submission to the dissertation office and graduation.

Major Events with Dates*

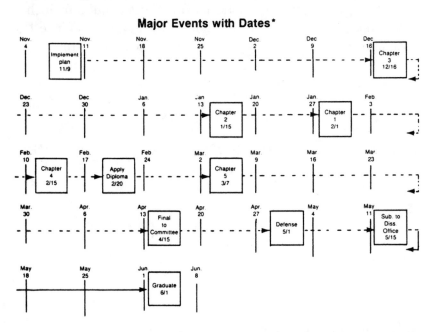

Your Sub-Activities with Dates

Drop down below the Dissertation Submission line. From your lists identify the CRITICAL activities and dates. These are the final activities on each list, i.e., Write Sample Section. Draw a box in the appropriate week for each of these activities

*Actual chart should be only one line across the top of a long sheet of paper.

and fill in the name and completion date. Now, check to be sure that the activities represented by the bottom set of boxes are to the LEFT of the appropriate activities in the top row. For example, Chapter 3, Methodology, cannot be turned in until the data collection, analysis, and sample sections are written. This is the time to identify constraints—in other words, what you have to do before you can do something else. Usually at this point you have to start adjusting dates. The dates you don't want to adjust are the ones for the defense and graduation. When you have all the boxes, connect those that are dependent on other activities with solid lines. Solid lines are drawn to indicate an event that must be completed before another event can be completed. Draw dotted lines to indicate that the completion of an activity is not dependent on the completion of another activity. For example, writing the data analysis description section is an activity that is independent of writing the data collection description section. (See also Introduction, page xviii, for sample chart.)

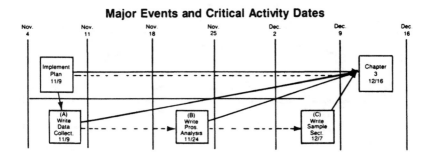

Major Events and Critical Activity Dates

Your Final Work Plan

Now, take one of your lists of activities and write in the activities in the columns between the appropriate dates. Use the list code (A1, C3, etc.) and a four- or five-word description. Activities can be combined, for example, "A1, 2, 4, 8, 9 Calls to arrange for sample." You still have your list to reference for details. You just want enough words so *you* know what *you* mean. When you have entered all of the activities from list A,

109

then enter all the activities from lists B, C, D, etc. Some lists will be sequential left to right; for example, all the activities on your list E will be completed before all the activities on your list F. In other cases, activities in a column will be drawn from several lists. However, it is essential that all activities that need to be completed prior to a critical date appear to the left of that date. At this point you may find it necessary to adjust many of the activity dates on your lists.

If you have computer application skills, there are several PC computer programs available that allow you to network your dissertation plan with similar results; however, you will have to weigh the cost in time and funds against the several hours it will take to do the job by hand.

Major Events, Critical Activity Dates, and Activities by the Week

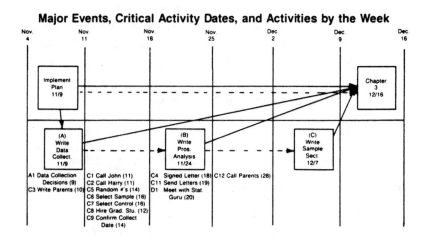

Twenty Days to Done!

You have your plan and your models for what the sections will look like. Your proposal has been approved and your time line accepted. Now all you have to do is collect, analyze, and WRITE. The collection and analysis is built into your time line at given points. The writing starts now! At a page an hour you can do 100 pages in 14.29 seven-hour workdays. Some of the pages have already been drafted for the proposal; all you may need to do for those pages is to change future to past tense. Based on 14.29 days for the first draft, you still have 5.7 days comfortably to make any changes suggested by your advisor or committee. If you have planned your dissertation for fifty pages, divide the number of days by two. In other words adjust the writing time frame to the planned length of your dissertation. Don't start off with an attitude of "Well, it will take up to twenty days"—figure out your workdays.

It is very helpful if you can set up a war room for the entire period of the dissertation—a place where you can get organized and begin and end work quickly. If possible, put your plan up on the wall. Check off in red every time an activity is completed. In a loose-leaf notebook set up dividers for each chapter and each heading.

Unlike a novel, which requires fluid transitions, the dissertation is broken up with lots of headings. Within a heading only simple transitions are needed paragraph to paragraph. What you write on a particular day will depend on (1) what you are ready to write and (2) your time line of critical events. For example, schedule writing the method sections for times when you are preparing to collect data and right after it is collected. If you are missing a piece of information, leave a blank and go back later when you have the information. As much as possible, you want to get things together for a section and then finish that section off. If support items will be part of the appendix, label them and put them in the notebook under Appendix ___ (unless they are "originals," in which case you place them in a folder labeled for copying). Much time can be wasted by having to go back to look up a citation or find a copy of some printout.

The Library

Plan trips to the library carefully. It is a myth that you have to spend your life in the library. Go to the library for specific and multiple purposes. For example, you have two summaries of literature searches on one of your three literature search topics: you go to the library to (1) get copies of the key studies you have identified and (2) to do a computer topic search for recent studies. On the same visit you get a book with a random number table for your method section, and you use the interlibrary loan program to order two books you need for another section of your literature search. Never just go to the library for the sake of going to the library. Almost as much time is wasted in the library by most graduate students as is wasted on selecting a topic. They go to the library and just start reading anything related to the topic and producing piles of useless note cards. Remember, you are probably going to write only a few pages on a topic; you want to identify what is relevant to your hypotheses and what is quality research. Know why you are collecting it and exactly how you are going to use it.

Work and Play

When you set up your activity lists, you built in time to write. Check the times to be sure they work out to a finished document. Also, in planning your writing or any other activity, remember that all work and no play will make you crazy. Don't schedule a seven-hour day of writing. Most people can only write for a couple of hours at a time. A day's schedule might be 9 A.M.: organize note cards on Topic A, read the two most recent studies; 10:30 A.M.: write 1.5 pages, 7 paragraphs on the topic; 12 Noon: eat lunch and take a walk; 1 P.M.: write the results section for hypotheses 2 (3 pages, 9 paragraphs); 4 P.M.: select the printouts to be included in the appendix, place them in a folder, and label them; 5 P.M.: shower and get ready to go out to dinner. Trying to schedule twelve-hour days or all-work weekends is an invitation to frustration and a feeling of failure. Your productivity drops off drastically if you focus on one thing too long, and you panic because you are falling behind. Plan, but plan to do less in a given period and you will get it done. You will be satisfied with your success and ready to tackle the next piece of work. All the work doesn't have to be done on weekends. If you work full-time, you may be really tired in the evenings; however, you may have the energy to write some short section, even a couple of paragraphs. These short writing bouts can total up quickly as you add them to the loose-leaf book. Evenings can also be used for grunt work: picking up items at the library, proofing work done by the typist, editing previously written pages. You want to save your non-employment workdays for major writing activities and fit in low-level activities during your less productive periods. Of course, for some "night people" it is the period after 9 P.M. when they can really write up a storm. To each his own!

Be sure to build in rewards and punishments. If you work all day on the dissertation, reward yourself in the evening. If you get ahead of schedule, take a day and do something exciting. If you get behind, fit in additional short work periods or take a "vacation day" from work and do dissertation work. If you have trouble keeping to a schedule, give your schedule to a "nudge" and make sure they nudge you!

Touching Base with the University, Your Advisor, Your Committee

You have an approved proposal and an agreed-to time line; however, don't disappear from sight. Plan both formal and informal contacts with your department, advisor, and committee. On the formal side, call or drop in to confirm that you will have that next chapter to read on the date planned and would like to set up an appointment to discuss the chapter on a specific day. Keep confirming your time line. Don't assume that your committee will remember. Don't expect that if something comes up in their schedule that they will remember to call you to reschedule.

You have to remember that they are professors and have professional as well as personal commitments. For example, if you know the professor will be away during the semester break, you may want to get a commitment that if you get him Chapters 1 and 2 three weeks before the end of the semester that he will meet with you and return them the week before the semester ends. Don't show up just before the semester break and expect your advisor to take your chapter with him/her to a meeting in Europe.

If you are having trouble with some aspect of the research, make an appointment and discuss it with your advisor or a member of the committee. This is the kind of help that you should be able to get, and it also gets them more involved in the project.

There is also an informal but absolutely important side of maintaining contact with the department, advisor, and committee. Remember this is also a "rite of passage." There is a certain amount of pain and suffering expected from a graduate student. You need to let them know how hard you are working. Let them know about the "late nights at the library" (make sure the library was open on the selected nights or be general). You want them to know that you are interested in what is going on in the department, what new research is being done, how their grant projects are going. You want them to know you are part of their world. You can do this by dropping in at times when you know members of the committee and department will be around. Stop by and see the secretaries in the department. Show up at the Christmas Party.

Getting Step-by-Step Advisor and Committee Approval—Surprises Are for Birthdays

The department or your advisor may have a specific process for the review of chapters as they are completed. In some cases the advisor and committee will really approve each chapter as it is completed; revisions are submitted until there is agreement. In other cases only the advisor needs to review the chapters. Your goal should be to get as much approval as possible as you go along. Your advisor may be the one designated to "approve" the work in progress, but hopefully you will be able to get other committee members to review and give input. If they give input and you revise, try to get them to review the revision. It is terribly important that you understand their input. Is what they are giving you a suggestion they think you might want to include, or is this a "suggestion" you better include or else? If you don't know, ask!

114

Sometimes, you just have to take a chance. For example, a committee member suddenly takes a trip at a critical time in your time line, and you can't get his input. Sometimes your advisor can cover for the committee member. If your advisor frequently works with this committee member on dissertations, he/she is likely to know the probable reaction. Sometimes even another graduate student may be able to alert you to items in a draft chapter, which the committee member may take exception to or want in more detail. However, weigh peripheral advice carefully.

When you have received input concerning a chapter and decided what changes will be made because they must be made and which ones you will make because they are politic to make and which changes you really agree should be made, make the changes as quickly as possible. Confirm with your advisor/committee that the changes were made. If the changes are extensive, have the chapter reviewed again.

The objective is to have no surprises in the defense or last minute rewrites. However, the goal is to finish on time! In reality you may have to balance the objective against the goal.

Summary

This chapter focused on getting organized and planning in great detail the actual writing of the dissertation. Activity lists were developed, critical events and times identified, and writing was scheduled. Becoming a drudge was discouraged. The need for visibility, controlled pain and suffering, and step-by-step approvals were discussed. The dissertation was written.

CHAPTER 7

DEFENDING THE DISSERTATION—TWO HOURS TO DOCTOR!

Variations on the Theme

There are a number of formats that schools use for conducting dissertation defenses. In some the defense is conducted by the three- or four-member committee that has "worked" with the student during the development of the dissertation. Other members of the department may be invited but, in practice, are unlikely to attend. Some schools add two or more specific staff members, either from the department or from outside, to the defense committee. These "significant others" receive copies of the dissertation and are expected to be involved actively in questioning. In some schools other graduate students routinely attend the defense. The variations in the structure of the defense is more a matter of differences in form than in substance. In other words, while the cast of characters may differ, the script is usually quite similar.

In the case where the dissertation committee and the defense committee are one and the same, you may find it easier to anticipate and plan for specific questions. However, by doing your homework you should be able to get a pretty good handle on where "new members" will be coming from. Whatever form your school uses, you are stuck with it, good or bad!

The Successful Defense

When you walk into the room for the defense, you want to be as relaxed and prepared as possible. If you have done your homework, this part of the process can be exciting and satisfying. If you have one or two "turkeys" on the committee, you may

117

have to settle for "miserable but successful." Success comes on a continuum. At one end, your advisor invites you back into the room following the post-defense conference, shakes your hand, calls you Dr. _____ , and tells you to just drop off the signed dissertation in the dissertation office. At the other end of the success continuum, the advisor invites you back into the room, shakes your hand, calls you Dr. _____ , and then the committee tells you about all the major changes you have to make, changes that will have to be approved by the advisor and/or committee members. Your experience will probably fall somewhere in the middle. Very few people get away with absolutely no changes or additions. Usually, as a minimum, a chart needs to be added or the description of X, Y, or Z needs to be expanded. These are things that can be done in a few hours. On the other hand, if you have worked closely with your committee, paid attention to their advice, and paid attention to the "rites of passage," major changes are also unlikely to be required. At this point in the process, the magic words are Dr. _____ . Even if there are a few hurdles left, you have won! The chances for winning are very high at the defense stage of the game. Remember your committee has invested hours (their perception may be that they spent months or years) in review and meetings. They have said publicly that your dissertation is ready to defend. They have a stake in your success. You really have to "blow" it on your end to have your dissertation rejected. Occasionally, a student is so poor in the defense that changes and a second defense are required. Forget the non-success options. Concentrate on success with minimum changes. Notice the goal is not "success-no-change." This is a nice bonus, but if you become too determined to get through with no changes, you may become belligerent in the defense and back a committee member into a wall, an absolute "no-no!"

Predicting the Questions to Be Asked in the Defense

There are at least three sources of information for determining in advance the questions you are likely to be asked in the defense: (1) your advisor or committee members tell you what they will ask; (2) your analysis of previously asked questions, comments, and interests of your advisor/committee; and (3) other students and graduates. The first is the most direct and any information gleaned from this source is likely to be accurate. You gather the information by asking for the information. By the time you get to the defense you have completed most of the rites of passage. Your advisor and committee have agreed that you are ready for the defense. The advisor and the committee have a stake in your project and your success. They don't want you to fall on your face in front of their colleagues. Also the dissertation defense is not like an exam in the traditional sense, since question security is not a major concern. Meet with your advisor for the specific purpose of discussing preparation for the defense. In most cases you will be told that the advisor's first statement at the defense will be: "Please give us an overview of your study." Focus on each section of the dissertation and discuss which areas might be of concern or "interest" to members of the committee. From this meeting you can develop a list of potential questions and identify who is likely to ask each question.

The second source for predicting what questions you will be asked is your own memory of past interactions with committee members. Go through your dissertation and recall any questions raised during the draft stage. These may be questions that you addressed in the final paper or ones that you decided to ignore. They may be handwritten notes made by committee members on drafts, which raised issues but did not require responses or changes in the dissertation. For example, your study involves primary school students; however, you find a note that says, "I wonder if this would be true of older students?" Obviously, the committee member did not intend for you to redo the study with older students; however, a question in the defense might be, "Do you think your findings would be the same with older students?" You will not have your own empirical evidence on which to base a response, but you may be able to cite a study that dealt with this population and be able to "predict" the "probable outcome" of a study with older students.

119

The third source of information are people who have gone through the defense with members of your committee or other graduate students who have attended defenses with those members. Using your study of dissertations completed in your department, it is relatively easy to identify and contact a graduate or two who went through a defense with each member of your committee. If new people have been added to your committee for the defense, it is particularly important to get information about them. Call identified graduates and ask for their advice on preparing for your defense. What kinds of questions were asked? What role did the committee member play in the meeting? In schools where graduate students routinely attend defense sessions, you should be able to find students who have attended sessions with each member of your committee and get the scoop on types of questions and the roles members played in the meeting. For example, "Professor Jones didn't ask any questions concerning other studies or the findings, but asked several questions concerning why certain methods were used to gather data. However, he was not antagonistic and seemed willing to accept the student's relatively simple response." If students attend dissertation defenses, you may be able to gather direct information by attending one or more sessions for other students, where your advisor or members of your committee are present. Following is a sample of how you might want to organize your information.

SAMPLE: DEFENSE ROLE/QUESTION IDENTIFIER FORM

Advisor

Role: After initial request for overview of study, sits back and lets others ask most of the questions; however, near the end, she asks questions that allow the student to provide strong responses, then brings the session to a close. Will interrupt if someone goes too far afield.

Possible Questions:

Please elaborate on how you feel your findings would have relevance for school curriculum.

How do you account for the fact that in the early studies in this area the findings were very different from those in your study and those of Johnson?

You have given some suggestions for future studies. Based on your findings, what do you think would be the outcome of those studies?

Committee Member #1: Professor Turkey

Role: Doesn't seem to be prepared. Leafs through dissertation while others are asking questions. Finally, zeros in on some small area that has never been raised as a concern and pounds it to death. In the end the student usually has to add a chart or clarifying sentence to the dissertation to satisfy this person. Once he gets his pound of flesh, he seems satisfied and doesn't participate further. Don't get into a fight with him.

Possible Questions:

Why did you limit your study to three case studies? Why not four or five?

I don't understand the heading on the chart on page 32, wouldn't it be clearer if it was labeled "X, Y, Z"?

Preparing the Answers for Your Defense

Once you have identified the potential questions and predicted the role each member of your committee will play, you are ready to think about your answers. The operative word here is "think." Consider what your response will be if the question is asked. At this point you know more about your little area of the field than anyone else in that room. It may be a narrow topic, but you really are the expert. Take each question and list two to five points you would make in a response. It is NOT advisable to write out in detail your answer. First, the question asked may vary slightly from the one for which you carefully developed a response, causing you to panic or answer the wrong question. Second, the defense is really a discussion with soon-to-be colleagues. You don't want it to appear that you have to read or repeat from memory any answers on your own work.

121

Third, if you try to memorize answers, it is likely that under the stress of the defense you will go blank. Fourth, the questions for the most part will be "Why?" or "What do you think?" questions, not ones you will need notes to answer.

Having said skip the notes as a crutch in the defense, there can be a couple of exceptions. First, if previous studies fall into two or more camps, a list of pro and con names may free you from worrying about whether under pressure you will forget. Such a list might look like the following:

SAMPLE: OTHER STUDIES

Pro	Population	Con	Population
Smith	4 yr olds	Jones, B	9 yr olds
Foster	Prisoners	DeSal	Special Ed
Smith/Lee	5/6 yr olds		
Gorden	High School		
Jones, L	4 yr olds		

Another exception might be in the field of statistics if this is an area where you feel uncomfortable. In preparing for the defense it is wise to touch base again with your statistical guru. Have her review one more time what you have written concerning the analysis. Have it explained to you again why this test and not some other was used. Make up a simplified card for reference. Such a card might look like the following:

SAMPLE: ANALYSIS PROCEDURE

Hypothesis	Test	Why
1. Age = thinking	Product Moment Correlation	Large sample, standardized test, normally distributed data. Ref: Winer

2. 4 yrs vs 6 yrs   Mann-Whitney U   Small sample, can rank,
                                  Difference   two independent groups.
                                                                Ref: Siegel

What you place on the card should be very short, just enough to trigger your memory. The entire hypothesis is not written out, just the briefest reference to what is compared. The main book reference is just the author's last name.

The final written crutch may be a list of hypotheses and findings. This would only be necessary if you have several hypotheses, which committee members may refer to or you may want to find in a hurry. The hypotheses card might look like the following:

SAMPLE: HYPOTHESES/FINDINGS

Hypotheses		Findings
H1	Age = Thinking	Correlation .77, Sig. .01
H2	4 yr olds vs 6 yr olds	Statistical dif. Sig. .05
H3	4 yr olds vs 5 yr olds	No statistical dif
H4	4 yr olds vs 3 yr olds	No statistical dif
H5	Sex = thinking	Correlation .82, Sig. .01

A Last Look at the Competition

It is extremely, extremely unlikely that someone else has been working on exactly the same study as yours and will publish their results just before your defense. However, it is likely that a related study, which supports or does not support some of your findings, has been published since the time you finished your literature search. It is not unreasonable to expect someone in the defense to ask you, "What do you think of the X, Y, Z study done by Anderson?" This is particularly true if such a study

123

received a lot of publicity. Remember, this is also a rite of passage—you are supposed to have a continuing interest in your topic and the field. One way to take out insurance on questions of this type is simply to pay a visit to the library and check for recent related studies. A last computer search may be worth doing if there is a lot of action in your field. You may find one or two related studies. Note differences and similarities of method and findings and if and how the findings support or conflict with your results. In these related studies you can almost always point out how their findings support yours or, because of methodology or population, their results don't contradict yours. You may find a couple of articles that have titles that sound related but really are not. In these cases, list the titles and just a few words to show why they are related to something else. Chances are no one at the defense will ask about any of these studies, but the couple of hours spent is worth the peace of mind.

If you have been in touch with any of the researchers who are working in your field on related studies, now is the time to touch base again. Find out what progress is being made on current studies. Are there any new studies underway? When asked about concurrent research or your interpretation of someone else's findings, it is impressive and further evidence of your interest in research to be able to respond, "I talked to Gloria Jones about the interpretation of her findings and she does perceive them as I have presented them" or, "Gloria Jones, at U of UCP, is working on a major study of X. Her findings will be interesting; however, she predicts her findings will be consistent with mine."

The Final Preparation

When you walk into the defense, you want to appear alert, modestly confident, and relaxed. In the real world, no one who is not certifiably crazy is going to be totally relaxed walking into the defense. However, with some preparation you can appear relaxed and, in fact, not be on the verge of a nervous breakdown. Good planning and organization are the keys that will give you a sense of being in control. As a result, stress will be reduced but not eliminated.

Find out what room will be used for the defense. Check it out. Sit in the chair you will sit in on the day of the defense. Is it particularly hot or cold? Is there a blackboard, a transparency projector, a screen? Is there a table for the committee, but rows of chairs for other observers or participants? Role-play in your mind what spending a couple of hours in this room will be like. If you can't find out until the last minute which conference room your defense will be in, visit all the possibilities.

Decide exactly what you are going to wear. What is the expected dress code for the defense in your school? This is not the time to make a counter-fashion statement. What your professors wear every day may or may not be a clue to how they will expect you to present yourself. They may live in jeans and sweaters; however, if your degree is in administration, business, psychology, etc., they will expect you to look like you're ready to enter the world of work outside the university. Remember, this is the last step in the rite of passage. Your clothes help you make the statement that you are ready. In most cases a suit will be appropriate. You also want to select clothes that will be comfortable. This means neat and pressed but probably not new. Try on the clothes you choose and visualize yourself in the room where the defense will take place. Will they be comfortable? Too hot? Once you have decided, have the outfit cleaned, have heels repaired on shoes, if necessary, and then set the entire outfit aside, so on *the day* you will not have to think about what you will wear.

You have probably bound your dissertation in a spring-loaded cover for your committee. This is an advantage in that it is hard for them to open it or keep it open to a particular page. However, you want to be able to find any page they make reference to quickly and keep the page open without fumbling. A three-ring binder serves well as your working copy of the dissertation. It works even better if you use dividers for each chapter and even subdividers for important sections. For example, a divider can be inserted before the results for each hypothesis or an important chart that summarizes findings. Tape your summary note cards to the back of the divider so that it faces the longer version of the information. Preparing your working copy of the dissertation in this format will allow you to find any section quickly and will eliminate sorting through note cards. The outline for your initial presentation can be placed at the beginning of the book. Finally, you can go through and underline or highlight in color major points in each section. Knowing that you will be able to find information quickly will help to reduce stress. It is also neater. You walk in, take one loose-leaf book from your attache case, place it alone on the table—you look prepared. Also, if your hands are shaking, it is less noticeable with a notebook than when you are sorting through cards or trying to hold a page open and talk at the same time. In your attache case is the regularly bound, pristine copy of your dissertation, which you will produce at the end of the defense for signatures.

Almost every defense begins with a request to give an overview of your study, usually ten to fifteen minutes. Again, you don't want to write this out and memorize it, but you do want to be prepared. Develop an outline of the major points and add to the outline key names and numbers. Use large type designed for presentations and use color underlining, maybe a different color for each section, to help you keep your place. Make the outline of your presentation the first section in your loose-leaf book. If you are in a field where overhead projectors are used for presentations—e.g., education, business—consider using an overhead in the defense. Your transparencies will provide the outline visually. The committee will focus on the screen, not on you, and you have the outline of your presentation right in front of you. If you go this route, check with your advisor to see if he approves. If you get the go-ahead, be sure to make or have made quality transparencies, with big print and very limited information on each transparency. Be sure to practice with the transparencies, if at all possible in the room where the defense will take place. On the day of the defense have two projectors in the room in case one fails. Whether you use transparencies or use the outline in your book, practice your presentation alone and in front of an audience. The audience may be friends who know at least something about your field, other graduate students, or just friends with a college education. Based on your presentation, any reasonably intelligent person should understand what you did, why it was important, what you found, and what your conclusions were. If your school encourages staff or other students to attend and participate in the defense, your presentation may be the only preparation they have for asking questions. The clearer the presentation, the less likely they are to ask unrelated or inappropriate questions.

SAMPLE PRESENTATION OUTLINE

I. Introduction

Big Problem:
- Single/working parents need day care
- Cost to society
- Effect on children—social behavior, future learning

What is known:
- X million single/working parents
- Cost to public—X billion
- Effects on children—little formal research, mixed results on social behavior and learning

Gap:
- Effect of specific types of day care on social development and learning readiness

Importance:
- Type of professional training
- Type of day care
- Cost

My Study:
- Comparison of two specific types of day care on social development and learning readiness, with implications for cost to society

II. Two Common Models of Day Care

Staff:
1. Professionals—5–6 ratio—each professional with a group
2. Professional/aides—5–6 ratio—professional works with aides who work with children

127

Cost: 1. $X
                   2. $X—Y

Program content: the same for both

Other Studies:

With Professionals—Johnson, Smith, and Strenger found equal social development and learning of children in day care and those at home.

With Aides—Gill, Harvey, and Ferrell found no negative effects on social development and learning of children in day care and those at home.

Robinson and Jessel found greater social development with aides than with professionals.

McCarthy and Lochten found greater learning with professionals than aides.

Conclusion: a mixed bag

My Hypothesis:

Learning readiness and social development will be equal under both methods; therefore, the professional/aide model is favored because of lower cost and availability of staff.

Limitations: • Children 3–5, in day care only two years
                   • Suburban children with parents with at least high
                     school education
                   • One type of program
                   • Limited sample size

III. Methods

                   • Sample—two matched groups—SES, Education
                     of parents, race, years in day care, IQ
                   • Professionals—all graduates of the same program
                   • Aides—all high school graduates, two weeks of
                     specific training

Data collected: • X, Y Social Index, Jones Parent Rating Form
                   • UV Reading Readiness
                   • Gils Math Readiness Index

Other data used: • National Day Care Report
                   • IQ records at each center
                   • Parent information forms at each center

IV. Findings:

- No dif. X, Y Social Index, or Jones Rating Form
- No dif. reading or math readiness

V. Conclusions:

- No statistical difference, accept hypothesis
- Cautions: Before changing training and public policy, replicate study with:
    1. other populations, e.g., poor urban
    2. other types of programs
    3. longitudinal studies

Finally, the traditional advice for preparing for any exam holds for preparing for the defense. Don't cram, go to bed early, and get a good night's sleep. If you haven't read some article or checked out something by five o'clock on the day before "D Day," forget it. Plan a peaceful evening, read a mystery or a trashy novel; just before you go to sleep, read through your presentation outline once and then go to sleep.

The Defense—Listen, Respond, Shut Up

You are prepared and the time has arrived—D Day, D Hour. In most cases after your committee and advisor arrive and you are all seated at the table, you will be asked to leave the room for a few minutes. This time allows the chairperson to discuss how the defense will proceed. For example, your advisor will tell the committee that he or she has asked you to give a brief overview of your study. Following the presentation they will go around the table for questions, taking each chapter in order. After the questions related to each chapter, there will be a chance to ask additional questions related to any part of the dissertation. When you come back into the room, it is not unusual for the chairperson to share with you the agreed-upon procedures. However, once your presentation is over, the questioning may or may not proceed as agreed upon. Someone hears your response to a question and jumps in with another question related to a different section of the study. Relax and go with the flow.

It is really important to listen to the questions. Don't jump to the conclusion that you know where the person is going and cut him/her off. Let the committee member state the entire question and make any elaboration related to the question. Listening carefully will ensure that you answer the question asked. Long elaborated questions also take up time when you don't have to talk. Remember, this has to take at least an hour, but rarely more than two, including the pre- and post-committee conferences.

Answer the question asked and *stop*. This is the advice old Washington hands also give to neophytes who are testifying as expert witnesses in Congress. In your enthusiasm don't get led into elaborating your findings into generalizations your study and data can't support. Frequently, committee members will ask leading questions to see how you will respond. Don't be defensive or back a committee member into a corner, no matter how off-the-wall the question or comment. If you don't understand the question, ask that it be repeated or you repeat what you think was asked. If you don't know the answer, say "That's an interesting question. I don't know the answer, but it would make a great study." If you flub-up on a question, forget it and concentrate on the next question.

During the questioning you will also get a sense of what changes or additions are going to be requested. Remember, it is unlikely that you will not have to make any changes; the goal is to have to make minimal changes and for the committee to say, "Congratulations, Dr. _____." It is possible in many cases to control the direction of required changes. For example, Professor K thinks that your summary data chart is confusing and would be better presented in some other given way. This is an easy change to make. Agree with him; tell him it makes more sense to do it that way. Sometimes a professor goes off on a tangent and really suggests what would amount to another whole study. You can try a response like, "That is a very interesting point. I agree it should be added to the section on recommendations for further research." Then shut up and look at another committee member or your advisor, ready for the next question. This strategy frequently works. Professor Y

130

really just wants to show how much he knows about the subject and doesn't expect you to do the study he proposes. You have recognized the merit of his position and accepted the idea as fitting into a specific section of your dissertation. You have provided a win-win response.

Sometimes, after a long rambling comment that does not include any clear question, a response of "That is an interesting point," followed by silence, will get you off the hook. At all costs you want to avoid win-lose contests. You may want to respond, "That is the dumbest question I ever heard; if you had read the dissertation you couldn't possibly ask such a question." It is perfectly possible that the idiot has not read your dissertation, just skimmed it or didn't read the major changes he required you to make after draft one. Find a way to focus your answer so neither of you have to lose. Remember where the power is. You may be able to point out a revised section and say something like, "I have added to the explanation in that section; maybe another paragraph on page 33 would add further to the clarity." If a member of the committee gets completely out of hand, it is likely that your advisor will come to the rescue. In one case, it was clear that a committee member had not read the final dissertation at all. All his questions related to the draft. The student made several statements related to changes in the draft, but to no avail. The chairman interrupted and asked the student to leave the room; when she returned five minutes later, the problem professor kept silent for the rest of the defense and made no suggestions for changes.

Finally, the chairperson will draw the defense to a close. Frequently the signal that the end is coming is a loaded question from your advisor, which will finish the defense off to your advantage. The chairperson then asks you to leave the room. The ten to thirty minutes outside the room are the worst. Inside the room you are being put into a category on the success continuum and the committee is deciding what changes you will have to make and who will approve them. It is getting agreement on the changes to be required that takes the time.

The tendency when the chairperson comes out and shakes your hand and calls you Dr. _____ is to go into shock.

Shock needs to be postponed for a few more minutes. You will need to make notes on the changes to be made. Don't argue; you have won! The changes may sound worse than they are and usually just your advisor will have to sign off. In some cases suggestions made during the defense will have been forgotten or dropped by the time you get a list of changes and additions. Let sleeping dogs lie. Don't press for details at this point. You will set a meeting date with your advisor to iron out what needs to be done and to set a time line for making the changes and having them approved.

The last thing you need to do is to thank everyone for all their help throughout the process. Be gracious, even if your real feelings would lead you to kick some of them in the shins. If it is time for lunch, this may be the time to invite the committee or your advisor to celebrate with you (at your expense). It is amazing, but once they speak the words that indicate you have succeeded, your committee and advisor actually do look better.

One final caution—after the defense and the congratulations, driving a car or operating machinery is not recommended for at least an hour. The adrenaline gives out and you are lucky to be able to coordinate walking. Sit and have a nice quiet cup of coffee, or if you have lunch with your advisor/committee, let them drive or walk, and watch what you drink. You don't want to have an honesty attack and tell one of them what you really think.

Summary

This chapter brought you to Dr. _____ . The goal for the defense was set as, "being addressed as Dr. _____ , with minimal required changes." The structure of the defense was discussed. Procedures were identified for anticipating questions, developing answers, organizing materials, and presenting an overview. Suggestions were made concerning handling questions in the actual defense and for controlling the required changes. A warm-fuzzy conclusion to the defense was recommended.

CHAPTER 8

CELEBRATING, THE LAST REVISION, POSTPARTUM DEPRESSION

Celebrating the Blessed Event

It is virtually all over, if you have followed the suggested schedule; a little less than nine months have passed and you have given birth to a successful dissertation. It's time to celebrate.

The first celebration, the night of the defense, should be small and informal. It is not a good idea to plan a party for that night. The knowledge that "people" have planned to celebrate with you will put extra pressure on you during the defense. If you have trouble with a question, you will be thinking, "What if I fail and they don't call me Dr. _____. How will I be able to face them at the party?" Also, after the expenditure of adrenaline during the defense and the rush of high immediately after your triumph, you will be pooped. A nice quiet dinner out with a significant other is recommended. Don't finalize the plans in advance. After the defense, call the restaurant and make reservations in the name of Dr. _____ .

You definitely deserve to reward yourself or to reap the benefits of friends who want to plan a celebration; think about the options occasionally during the nine months of work, but make or accept no definite plans until after the defense. A survey of a substantial sample of Ph.D.'s and Ed.D.'s showed that the party given for or by friends was the most common form of celebrating, a kind of coming-out party. However, celebrating was not limited to one party. Some of the other forms of celebrating included

- reading five mystery books in a row
- having ears pierced

- buying a new wardrobe
- buying presents for those who helped
- buying season tickets to football games
- taking a trip
- taking the family on a trip
- changing professions
- buying an expensive piece of jewelry for the graduate's wife or husband
- having stationary printed with the new title
- updating the new doctor's transcript
- re-doing the living room

Most of the ways people celebrate seem to reflect a feeling of making up for perceived deprivation during the dissertation process.

The Last Revision

One of the hardest things to do is to get back into harness and make the final revisions and have the final copies made, bound, and delivered. It seems that the fewer the changes, the more apt you are to procrastinate. If your defense is only a week or so before the deadline date for submission of finished dissertations for spring graduation, the pressure is on. However, if your defense is in January and the final date is the end of April, it is easy to put off the last details. Build time into your schedule for final revisions when you plan your dissertation time line. Commit yourself to a specific date to deliver the final version to your advisor. Get your advisor to commit to a date to get back to you concerning his or her approval.

Right after the defense, set a date to meet with your advisor to review the needed revisions. A good time would be the beginning of the next week. This time line gives you a chance to think about and minimize the scope of the changes and gives your advisor time to forget some of the details of the changes required by other committee members. Make a list of the changes, with notes on what you plan to do for each. For example, add a chart showing the match between sample and con-

134

trol. The chart will have the following headings: Mean Age, Mean IQ, Mean Parent Education, Mean Years in Program. If the change is minor or is very clear, you may want to list the change and actually bring the change to the meeting for approval. Pay particular attention to changes required by your advisor, particularly if he/she is the only one who has to approve the changes. Your advisor may not have really agreed with changes others on the committee wanted; therefore, he/she is going to be less interested and rigorous about those changes. Your advisor may not even remember the full dimension of the changes required by others on the committee. When you make your list, you want to propose the "minimum" in actual changes. For example, if a section of the literature search was judged incomplete, you don't want to propose a complete re-write, instead you might suggest adding one or two specific new studies. At this final stage your advisor considers you virtually "done" and wants to wrap up the loose ends. This is to your advantage.

Actually, your advisor's main interest may be in your writing an article for submission to a journal based on your study or your co-authoring an article with your advisor. Don't reject these proposals out-of-hand. Being enthusiastic about the idea of publishing will make it easier to get the changes approved, and while any thought of writing is probably repulsive at this point, this may be your best chance to see your name in print. Take a break of a month or so and then write the article. You have all the information, you just need to change the format.

After meeting with your advisor and reaching agreement on the changes, make the changes and get them approved. Get the final copies made and get them bound. Complete the paperwork for having your dissertation published in *Dissertation Abstracts International*, as well as any paperwork for graduation. Turn everything in to the appropriate office.

Postpartum Depression

Warning! Completing a dissertation can be dangerous to your emotional health. Many graduates report strange symptoms following the doctoral celebrations. The person will sit down to read the paper and find that after a couple of minutes he/she is wandering around the house. Life doesn't seem as great as the new doctor thought it would be. Others in the graduate's life who were willing to postpone or forgo certain activities now expect enthusiastic participation or the doing of those things that have been put off.

There are no pills to cure the condition. However, recognizing that it is a syndrome shared by many graduates, at least, should assure you that you are not going "nuts." The good news is that the syndrome disappears in a short period of time with a return to a balanced state. What is a balanced state? It is a recognition that it was hard, regimented work, but it was worth it, Dr. _____ !

Summary

This chapter tied up the loose ends. Ideas for celebrating were suggested. The final revisions were made. The copies were delivered to the dissertation office. Postpartum depression was anticipated and assurance given that this negative state would be replaced in a short time with the feeling that it was all worth it!

REFERENCES

ANDERSON, M. 1992. *Impostors in the Temple*. New York, NY: Simon and Schuster.

CRONBACH, L. J. 1960. *Essentials of Psychological Testing*. Second edition. New York, NY: Harper and Brothers.

BROYLES, S. G. 1986. *National Center for Educational Statistics: Higher Education Annuals and Biennials*. Washington, DC: Statistical Abstract of the United States.

COOK, D. L. 1979. *Program Evaluation and Review Technique*. Lanham, MD: University Press of America.

EDWARDS, A. L. 1984. *Experimental Design in Psychological Research*. Fifth edition. New York, NY: Holt, Rinehart and Winston.

National Center for Educational Statistics, U.S. Department of Education. 1990. *The Condition of Education, 1990, Volume 2, Postsecondary Education*. Washington, D.C.

National Center for Educational Statistics, U.S. Department of Education. 1991. *The Condition of Education, 1991, Volume 2, Postsecondary Education*. Washington, D.C.

NAYLOR, P. D. and T. R. Sanford. 1982. "Intrainstitutional Analysis of Student Retention across Student Levels," *College and University*, 57(2): 143–159.

RUCH, F. L. 1959. *Psychology and Life*. Fifth edition. Chicago, IL: Scott, Foresman and Company.

SIEGEL, S. 1956. *Nonparametric Statistics for the Behavioral Sciences*. New York, NY: McGraw-Hill Book Co.

1968. *Webster's New World Dictionary of the American Lanaguage*. New York, NY: The World Publishing Co., p. 1304.

WINER, B. J. 1971. *Statistical Principles in Experimental Design*. Second edition. New York, NY: McGraw-Hill Book Co.

ABOUT THE AUTHOR

Dr. Evelyn Hunt Ogden received her doctorate in Educational Evaluation, Psychological Measurement and Statistics from Rutgers University. She is the author of major studies and reports and has served for many years on the U.S. Department of Education Program Evaluation Panel, which reviews and accepts or rejects research related to claims of program effectiveness.

As State Education Deputy Assistant Commissioner for Research, Planning, and Evaluation and as a consultant, she has worked successfully with scores of doctoral students from major universities in fields from education to biological science. Some were young full-time graduate students; most were older working part-time students; some were running out of university-imposed time; others had given up in the past and had decided to give it one last shot. The advice she gave them was unconventional, definitely not what was taught in dissertation seminars; however, it worked.